The Victorian Nursery Book

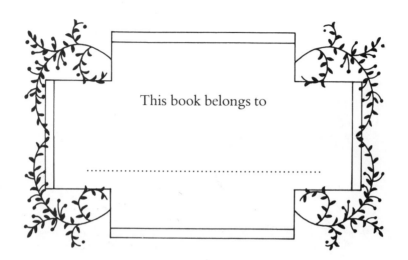

This book belongs to

....

The Victorian Nursery Book

Antony & Peter Miall

PANTHEON BOOKS, NEW YORK

For our mother

Library of Congress Cataloging in Publication Data

Miall, Antony.
The Victorian nursery book.

1. Children—Great Britain.   2. Nurseries.
3. Governesses.   4. Great Britain—Social life
and customs—19th century.   I. Miall, Peter.
II. Title
HQ792.G7M5   649′.1   81-47206
ISBN 0-394-51597-8   AACR2

By the same authors: THE VICTORIAN CHRISTMAS BOOK.

Manufactured in the United States of America
First American Edition

CONTENTS.

'Primavera'.

ACKNOWLEDGMENTS.

IN compiling *The Victorian Nursery Book* the authors have been helped enormously by many people who grew up in nurseries around the turn of the century and who recalled this period of their lives with affection or loathing, but always with clarity. To these people we should like to extend our warmest thanks. In a very real sense it is their book. To Captain Sir Cecil Boyd-Rochfort and his sister, Muriel McCall, whose childhood photographs appear in the Album section, we are indebted for their permission to reproduce them. In addition we should like to thank Jeremy Cooper for permission to photograph his magnificent collection of toys and the National Trust for permission to photograph the nursery at Wallington House. David Fawcett's splendid work on all the pictures has been a constant source of inspiration, and Elizabeth Bateman's searches on our behalf as well as her astounding memory have also been invaluable.

Finally, we should like to thank Judith Allen, Sabrina Izzard and the staffs of the London Library and the British Library for their help and, for constant support and helpful criticism, our several families.

ANTONY AND PETER MIALL

INTRODUCTION.

WHERE did you come from, baby dear?
Out of the everywhere into here.
But how did you come to us, you dear?
God thought of you, and so I'm here.

GEORGE MACDONALD (1824–1905)

GEORGE MACDONALD might well have been one of those Victorian fathers who neatly avoided questions about the facts of life by telling their offspring that babies arrived in those large black Gladstone bags which doctors always carried. In other parts of Europe embarrassed parents explained that boys and girls were dressed in blue and pink respectively because male children were found under cabbages and female ones in the hearts of roses. Considering the size of families in the nineteenth century and the frequency with which these fables must have been trotted out, it is amazing that so many children swallowed them whole.

Nevertheless, if Victorian children were ignorant of the facts of life, their parents were almost as ignorant of the medical facts of confinement, birth and baby-care. Up until the middle of the eighteenth century it was rare for more than a quarter of the babies born to survive infancy, and even as late as the 1850s nearly half the children born died before they reached their fifth year. Between June 1848 and July 1849, the total number of deaths in Birmingham was 3,305. Of these some 1,658 were of children under five and more than half of these died before their first birthday. There can be no doubt that ignorance was in large measure to blame for this state of affairs. Children were particu-

larly prone to contract any one of the many fatal or near-fatal
illnesses with which Victorian society abounded and for which
there was no adequate treatment – as many poets of the time were
moved to point out:

> Who bids for the little children,
> Body and soul and brain?
> Who bids for the little children,
> Young, and without stain?
> 'Will no one bid,' said England,
> 'For their souls so pure and white,
> And fit for all good or evil,
> The world on their page may write?'
>
> 'We bid,' said Pest and Famine,
> 'We bid for life and limb;
> Fever and pain and squalor
> Their bright young eyes shall dim.
> When the children grow too many
> We'll nurse them as our own,
> And hide them in secret places,
> Where none may hear their moan.'

ANON (1852)

Even towards the end of the century the rate of infant mortality was surprisingly high. In his book on the diseases of infants
and children published in 1891, E. Harris Ruddock provides a
formidable list of illnesses which could still be fatal: scarlet fever,
scarlatina, dropsy, measles, German measles, smallpox,
chicken-pox, typhoid, diphtheria, hooping cough, mumps,
rickets and many others. It is small wonder that a contemporary
book on household management devoted four chapters to 'A
Death in the Household'. There can have been few Victorian
families who had not followed at least one small coffin on its last
journey.

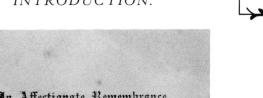

Memorial card for a Victorian child – 50 per cent of children
born in the mid-nineteenth century died in infancy.

A FUNERAL COSTING £53

Hearse and four horses, two mourning coaches with fours,
twenty-three plumes of rich ostrich-feathers, complete velvet
covering for carriages and horses, and an esquire's plume of
best feathers; strong elm shell with tufted mattress, lined and
ruffled with superfine cambric, and pillow; full-worked
glazed cambric winding sheet, stout outside lead coffin, with
inscription, plate and solder complete; one and a half inch oak
case, covered with black or crimson velvet, set with three
rows round, and lid panelled with best brass nails; stout brass

plate of inscription, richly engraved; four pairs of best brass handles and grips, lid ornaments to correspond; use of silk velvet pall; two mutes with gowns, silk hat-bands and gloves; fourteen men as pages, feathermen and coachmen, with truncheons and wands, silk hat-bands etc.; use of mourners' fittings; and attendant with silk hat-band etc.

That advertisement from a Victorian undertaker details his most expensive funeral – one unlikely to be mounted for a mere child. The 'parsell of sweete infancie' might only have merited a funeral costing £3. 5s. A plot in Nunhead or Highgate Cemetery for a child was priced at £1. 10s. and monuments started at £7. Finally the parents would have chosen an epitaph suitable for a child, of which there were plenty current in Victorian England:

> Scarce had I flutter'd into life,
> And joy to my dear parents given,
> Than on my tender brow was placed,
> A crown of righteousness in heaven.

> *Epitaphs for Country Churchyards,*
> AUGUSTUS HARE (1856)

And this was to be the fate of almost 50 per cent of mid-Victorian children. It is hardly to be wondered at that the literature of the period abounds in pathetic death-bed scenes and mawkish sentimentality where babies are concerned:

> 'What wakes me from my gentle sleep?
> Sweet sounds my soul delight:
> O mother, see! what can it be,
> At this late hour of night?'

> 'I nothing hear, I nothing see,
> So rest in slumber mild;
> No music comes to comfort thee,
> Thou poor and sickly child!'

INTRODUCTION.

'It is no earthly sound I hear,
That gives me such delight;
'Tis angels call me with their song –
So, mother dear, good night!'

ANON (1860)

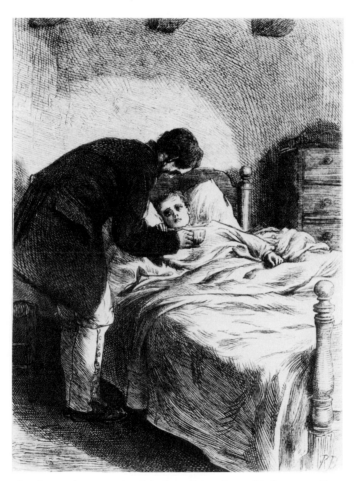

Sentimental portrayals of the horrifying facts of infant mortality
helped the Victorians to face up to them.

Equally, it comes as no surprise to find that the Victorians made an enormous fuss of a child's first birthday and that they observed the whole business of childhood with an almost religious interest. Sentimentality was, to our forefathers, a kind of safety valve – codifying their fears and pleasures into shareable experiences. Mortality, and especially infant mortality, was in a real sense the common enemy of nineteenth-century society.

On a more practical level, the Victorians counteracted mortality with an unparalleled enthusiasm. Between 1801 and 1911 the population of England and Wales grew by a staggering 11 per cent per annum. Large families were the norm. Edward Lear had twenty-one brothers and sisters, Charles Dickens had ten children and even the Queen herself had nine. Such large families needed a great deal of looking after and Victorian mothers began to find it difficult to cope single-handed with the little tribe of children which might well have included a Septimus, an Octavia and even a Decimus. Fortunately, improvements in medical science and a growth in general affluence provided a situation in which there were plenty of girls looking for jobs as nurses and plenty of families who needed them.

Finally, all these children and their nurses, nursemaids and nursery staff found their niche on the upper stories of large Victorian houses. There behind stout, soundproof doors and with safely barred windows, they made their little world – a special world of nursery books, toys, pictures, mealtimes, lesson times and walk times and, above all, a world pervaded by nursery lore and the nursery ethic. Here, 'nurse' – or 'nanny' as she became known at the end of the century – was Queen. Even parents were only visitors. So much depended upon her character and disposition. A good nurse could give her charges love and security. She could ease those traumatic moments in a child's life and prepare the way for adulthood while making childhood a rosy memory forever. A bad nurse could mar entire lives.

INTRODUCTION.

In a century when childhood becomes shorter and shorter and when children become little adults almost overnight, it is, perhaps, easier for us to understand the childhood of eighteenth-century children. These miniature grown-ups in their waistcoats, stockings and breeches knew little of childish ways and lived their early years in an adult world. While they swam almost from birth in the open sea, their grandchildren paddled away their formative years in the shallows. Just which of these two methods of upbringing was most effective is difficult to judge. But there is indubitably something reassuring and comforting in this glimpse of the soft and sepia world that was the Victorian nursery.

THE BABY.

ONLY a baby small,
Dropped from the skies;
Only a laughing face,
Two sunny eyes.

Only two cherry lips,
One chubby nose;
Only two little hands,
Ten little toes.

Only a golden head,
Curly and soft;
Only a tongue that wags.
Loudly and oft.

Only a little brain,
Empty of thought;
Only a little heart,
Troubled with nought.

Only a tender flower
Sent us to rear;
Only a life to love
While we are here.

Only a baby small,
Never at rest;
Small, but how dear to us,
God knoweth best.

'Only a Baby Small', MATTHIAS BARR (*c.* 1870)

THE young Victorian wife finding herself in 'a certain condition' would be inclined, unlike her twentieth-century counterpart, to keep the information very much to herself and her immediate family for as long as possible. Given her way of life this was much more feasible than it would be today. Nineteenth-century women's clothing was designed to conceal rather than to reveal, and the fact that a woman was not seen about so much might quite well pass unremarked. Provided that she took her exercise in a closed carriage and that her outings were confined to the hours of dusk, the first knowledge her friends and neighbours would have of the impending arrival would be the sight of the doctor making more frequent calls and, of course, the appearance of the monthly nurse.

The Victorian woman finding herself in 'a certain condition' followed the advice of medical journals of the day and rested frequently as her confinement approached.

What Queen Victoria referred to as 'the shadow side of marriage' was not discussed in polite society. There was no real ante-natal care and the mother-to-be would have had to resort to one of those discreet publications on 'women's matters' for any guidance she might have needed in the months leading up to the happy event:

> When a woman is about to become a mother, she ought to remember that another life of health or delicacy is dependent upon the care she can take of herself; that all she does will inevitably affect her child, and that mentally as well as physically.
>
> We know that it is utterly impossible for the wife of the labouring man to give up work, and, what is called 'take care of herself', as others can. Nor is it necessary. 'The back is

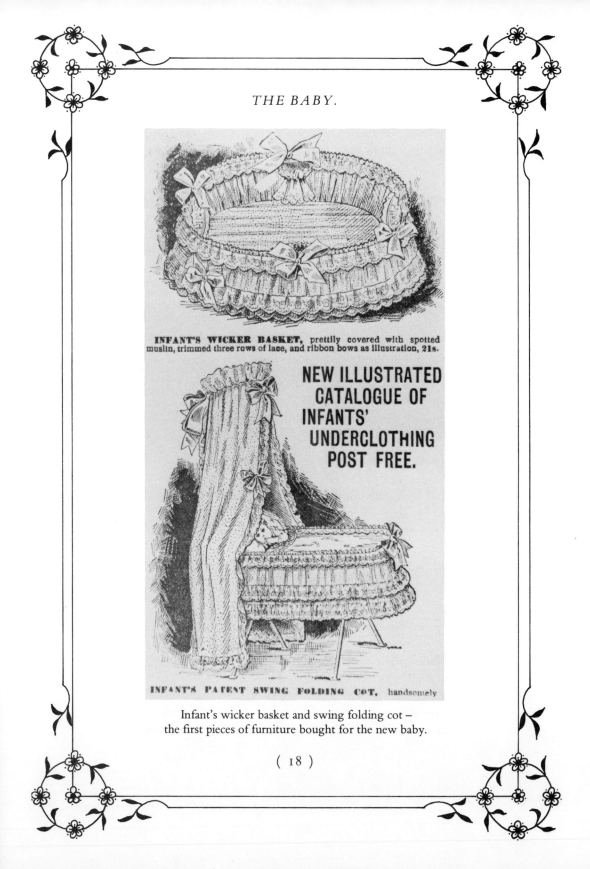

INFANT'S WICKER BASKET, prettily covered with spotted muslin, trimmed three rows of lace, and ribbon bows as illustration, 21s.

NEW ILLUSTRATED CATALOGUE OF INFANTS' UNDERCLOTHING POST FREE.

INFANT'S PATENT SWING FOLDING COT, handsomely

Infant's wicker basket and swing folding cot –
the first pieces of furniture bought for the new baby.

made for its burthen.' It would be just as injurious for the
labourer's wife to give up her daily work, as for the lady to
take to sweeping her own carpets or cooking the dinner...He
who placed one woman in a position where labour and
exertion are parts of her existence, gives her a stronger state of
body than her more luxurious sisters. To one inured to toil
from childhood, ordinary work is merely exercise, and, as
such, necessary to keep up her physical powers, though extra
work should be, of course, avoided as much as possible.
Lifting heavy weights, taking long walks, stooping for many
hours over a washing-tub – all these things might be avoided
or done in moderation even by a cottager's wife.

Cassell's Household Guide

The same Victorian manual goes on to advise the expectant
mother as to her diet during pregnancy; not for her the 'tea and
cakes and jam, and slices of delicious ham, and chocolates with
pink inside' that had so delighted Hilaire Belloc's Jim:

At such a time, too, the woman ought to be as careful as she
can of her diet, and eat regularly, and in moderate quantity.
Over-loading the stomach with too much rich food increases
the sickness so often attendant upon her state. The vulgar
notion of what is called 'longing' for unusual food should be
discouraged as inconsistent and ridiculous.   ibid.

So much for 'cravings'! – however, the young mother-to-be
must have taken much comfort from the no-nonsense approach
to her actual confinement as well as from the advice not to get up
too soon after the birth – another practice which differed widely
from today's:

It is a fatal error, very prevalent, however, in some classes of
society, that to get up soon is a sign of a 'clever woman'; and a
sort of rivalry exists upon the point – the mother who can
soonest 'feel her feet', and get to her usual work or business,

being looked up to and envied by her neighbours. There can scarcely ever be any necessity why a woman should get up and work under nine days, at least. Neighbours are always ready to come in and set the house to rights, or see to the children and the husband. Therefore, by all means, rest the prescribed nine days. Let nature perform her work her own way, and you will find your reward in an after-time of strength and comfort. We do not hesitate to affirm that, in nine cases out of ten, the rash and indecently early rising from child-bed is not from a sense of duty or necessity, but simply out of bravado. This period of after-repose is particularly required at a first confinement, the strength and health of the mother's whole life depending upon judicious treatment at such a critical time.

ibid.

Although it was customary for the middle-class mother-to-be to be assisted in the actual birth and its aftermath by a 'monthly' nurse, such a woman was only a temporary addition to the household. If there were no other children already, the whole business of engaging a permanent nurse had to be gone into. We shall see later just which qualities the lady of the household had to look for in the perfect applicant for this post. Having engaged the nurse, however, the young Victorian wife could settle down to a comparatively trouble-free confinement, always supposing that the two nurses between them could be relied upon to look after their employer as well as their younger charge:

> The great thing for a nurse to observe, after the baby is born, is to keep the mother's mind free from excitement or anxiety, and to observe as much quiet in the house as possible. In a healthy woman, Nature will do her own doctoring, and do it thoroughly; but when there is ill-health or debility, the nurse or doctor must help Dame Nature, and be in their turn attended to and assisted by those immediately connected with the patient.   ibid.

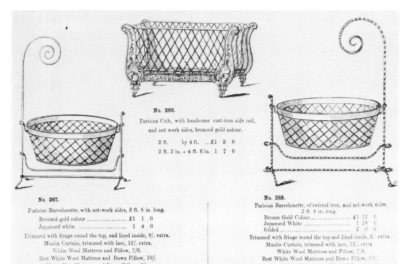

Parisian iron crib and cots – as advertised and sold by Heal's of London in 1853.

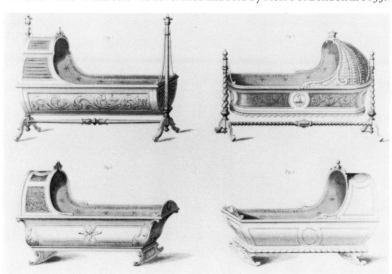

For the nobility and gentry – cot and crib designs from *The Cabinet Maker's Assistant* (1853).

THE BABY.

This surely must have been the most trying time for any Victorian mother – surrounded as she was by the monthly nurse, the resident nurse, the doctor and any other members of staff and family who might feel themselves needed in the dash to assist 'Dame Nature'. How she must have longed to be left alone with the cause of all the fuss!

> Baby, I lie and gaze on thee,
> All other thoughts forgot;
> In dreams the things of earth pass by,
> But awake I heed them not.
> I hear thy soft breath come and go,
> Thy breath so lately given,
> And watch the blue unconscious eyes,
> Whose light is pure from heaven.

Poems and Pictures, ANON. (1860)

This young Victorian mother has only just been allowed to come downstairs, but her sister is obviously delighted with the new addition to the family.

But such moments of calm were short-lived. All too soon one of the nurses would have been bustling back:

> The first thing, after washing and dressing, is to feed the child. Most babies make a sucking motion with their lips almost directly they come into the world, and ought to have their hunger gratified within a few hours. If the mother is not in a state to do this (as is very seldom the case under thirty-six hours), give the baby a little oatmeal gruel, very thin and smooth. Most nurses administer a couple of drops of castor-oil with this first meal. A baby for the first weeks requires to be very often fed – in fact, its existence consists of eating and sleeping. A healthy baby will generally, therefore, be a quiet one. If it fidgets and whimpers, there is something the matter. Screaming as often proceeds from temper as from pain, babies learning wonderfully soon to assert their rights; and, finding out that by crying they can get their desires gratified, crying is resorted to whenever they are thwarted. Never dose a baby with narcotics. Laudanum has a poisonous effect upon some infants – one drop having been known to produce death. The safest remedy for a pain in the stomach is a few drops of peppermint in water and sugar, and a hot flannel laid upon the stomach or across the back.

The ancient practice of giving a child to a wet nurse was well on the wane by the beginning of the nineteenth century and by the 1880s such a thing was almost unheard of. Most Victorian mothers suckled their own children and for those who could not for any reason, there was a bewildering array of patent feeding-bottles:

> Many new inventions in feeding-bottles have lately been introduced, few of which, in our opinion, can vie with the old-fashioned bottle, provided with an india-rubber nipple, or one formed of the calf's teat. This last requires more attention on the mother's part. She ought, in fact, to have two, and use

MELLIN'S FOOD
For Infants and Invalids.

" Heligoland, Oct. 1st, 1891.
"Mr. Mellin. Sir,—Permit me to enclose two photos of my little daughter, Etha, taken at the ages of 4 and 4½ months respectively. Two weeks after birth, finding her mother's milk insufficient, we tried your Food, with the result that on the first day a visible improvement was evident. She has continued taking the Food exclusively up to date, and now at the age of 9 months she is a robust and healthy girl, inducing all who require artificial help to use your Food with the same satisfactory results.
(Signed) "G. FRIEDERICHS."

MELLIN'S FOOD BISCUITS

(Manufactured by CARR & CO., Carlisle, specially for G. Mellin).
For Children after Weaning, the Aged and Dyspeptic.
Digestive, Nourishing, Sustaining
Price 2 - & 3 6 per Tin.

ETHA FRIEDERICHS.

MELLIN'S
LACTO-GLYCOSE or MILK FOOD.

Simply dissolved in warm water is recommended for use when fresh cow's milk disagrees or cannot be obtained. Price 2 - and 3 - per Bottle.

SHAKESPERIAN WISDOM ON THE FEEDING AND REARING OF INFANTS—A Pamphlet of quotations from Shakespeare and portraits of beautiful children, together with testimonials, which are of the highest interest to all mothers. To be had with Samples, free by post, on application to

G. MELLIN, Marlboro' Works, Peckham, London, S.E.

Mellin's Food – an advertisement for one of the many proprietary
brands of babyfood available to the Victorian mother.

them on alternate days, keeping that not in use in a little gin or whisky, and washing in warm water before putting it upon the bottle, where it must be very firmly tied with a piece of fine tape. The bottle so frequently used now, with the long india-rubber tube, no doubt saves the nurse a certain amount of trouble, but requires too strong a pull and strain from the tongue; besides, the food is apt to get cold, and cold food always gives the infant wind, and causes it to torment the mother by a fit of crying.

Another important part of both the baby's and the nurse's routine was the bath. Once again the ingenious Victorian inventor came to the assistance of the nursery staff with any number of

A nineteenth-century manual of baby-care suggests this method of bathing if the child shows an early aversion to the baby-bath.

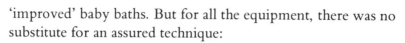

'improved' baby baths. But for all the equipment, there was no substitute for an assured technique:

> Careful washing night and morning is all important. The whole body must be well rubbed and soaped. Then put the child into the water, supporting its back with your left hand, having your fingers well spread out; rub off the soap with the right, and lave the water over the back and head; taking care never to frighten or force the child into the water; but, if on any occasion it shows an aversion to the 'ducking', coax it in, or even give it a wash only upon your knee, rather than risk exciting its fears.
>
> Every part must be carefully dried, especially the folds of the skin, as these, if left wet, are sure to chafe and become sores, often very difficult to heal. Violet-powder* is used to dust into these folds, but is worse than nothing unless the skin is perfectly free from damp. When washed, let the child stretch well, and lying flat upon your knees, enjoy its freedom from the trammels of clothing. A healthy child will always stretch and use its small limbs in a most energetic manner when naked; nor does it at all relish having itself dressed again. Always use rain or soft water, if you can get it, curd soap, and a bit of flannel made into a fingerless glove. Rub till the skin is in a glow, taking care not to ruffle or chafe it. In winter weather, a few drops of glycerine in the water will prevent frost-roughness or chapping, both entailing much suffering upon the little one, and at the same time capable of being avoided by proper care and attention.

A Victorian nurse was also expected to be a good needle-woman. It may be that the mother might have enjoyed making

---

*Royalists might have preferred *'The Sanitary Rose Powder' for Nursery and Toilet use as recommended by H.M. Queen Victoria*. The manufacturers avowed: 'The Queen says:– "It is a very superior article, fragrant, soothing and cleanly. We think it merits the praise given to it." '

baby clothes for the impending arrival, but repairing and adding to a child's wardrobe was one of the nurse's important duties. For advice on making a child's petticoat or skirt, she might have turned once again to *Cassell's Household Guide:*

We promised in our last number to lay before our readers practical directions for making babies' long frocks and petticoats. These are not worn so long in the skirt as they were formerly. For full-dress toilette for a baby the skirt of the robe, however, is still very long; and as the body, including the band, is two and a half inches deeper than the old-fashioned ones, the difference in length is not very great. The length of the skirt of a robe thirty or forty years ago was forty inches, and the body three inches. A full-dress robe is now made thirty-six inches long in the skirt, and five and a half in the body. It will be the best plan for the young mother to commence by making the petticoats before she attempts the frocks, by which arrangement she will get her hand accustomed to the work.

Half a dozen white petticoats and half a dozen plain frocks, with one or two handsomer for best, will be sufficient; but where means allow of frequent change, double the number can be made, and the every-day frocks embroidered also. For the petticoats, a fine, thin, soft long-cloth should be chosen, and will cost ninepence or a shilling a yard. Eleven yards will be sufficient for six petticoats; a very wide material is not needed. Also two pieces of tape, one a quarter of an inch, the other three eighths of an inch wide. The long-cloth not dressed should be procured. It can always be had by inquiring for it at a really good shop. The thrifty housewife will find that she saves ten or twenty per cent by going to a large, well-established shop, and the trouble and fatigue of a long walk, or the expense of an omnibus, will be amply repaid to her in the end. When a lady has to go a distance to a shop she should try and make all the purchases needed at once, which may easily be done by keeping a little memorandum-book and pencil in the pocket, and jotting down from time to time the articles in requisition.

The petticoat may be made in the following way – cut off nine breadths, of thirty-four inches each. Split three of these in half lengthways, to make half breadths. Each skirt consists of a breadth and a half. If the material is undressed, soaking is necessary. Rubbing between the hands or soaping the work with dry soap, is sometimes sufficient preparation if it is dressed. It should always be soaped for the sewing machine. Any dress in the material clogs the feeder and impedes the motion. If the work is soaked it should be ironed whilst damp, and made very smooth, otherwise it is not easy to work evenly upon it. Where the selvedges come the breadth and half-breadth of the skirt need only be run together neatly. The other seam must be run and felled.

Make a cut down the centre of the half-breadth, seven and a half inches long as shown at C in Fig. 33, and hem it round with the narrowest hem that can be turned down, neatly button-hole stitching the angle A, Fig. 32, and then making a loop across, shown at BBB. In case any of our readers are not acquainted with the correct mode of making a loop, we will describe it in detail, with the help of the diagram, Fig. 34. Pass the cotton from side to side two or three times, taking an imperceptible stitch through the material, and keeping the three bars of cotton as close together and as much like one as possible. Then work over them closely in button-stitch, as shown in Fig. 35. The object of this loop is to prevent the placket-hole from tearing down, and must be made to all the frocks as well as the petticoats.

Next hem round the skirt, as shown at D in Fig. 33, and then gather it finely at the top (E and E) all round. Gathering is simply running, and drawing up the thread. It will be necessary to use rather coarse cotton for this purpose, because a fine thread is always exceedingly liable to break in the drawing.

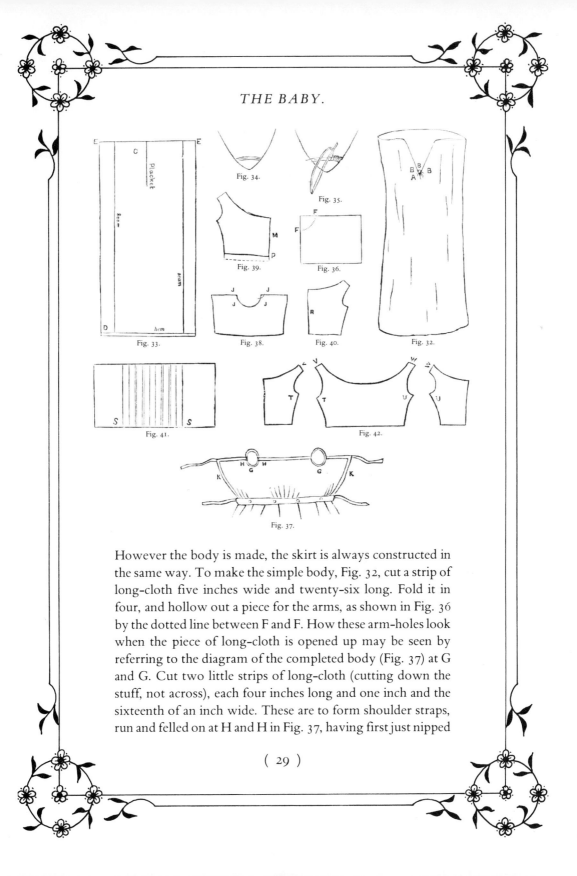

Fig. 34.

Fig. 35.

Fig. 39.

Fig. 36.

Fig. 33.

Fig. 38.

Fig. 40.

Fig. 32.

Fig. 41.

Fig. 42.

Fig. 37.

However the body is made, the skirt is always constructed in the same way. To make the simple body, Fig. 32, cut a strip of long-cloth five inches wide and twenty-six long. Fold it in four, and hollow out a piece for the arms, as shown in Fig. 36 by the dotted line between F and F. How these arm-holes look when the piece of long-cloth is opened up may be seen by referring to the diagram of the completed body (Fig. 37) at G and G. Cut two little strips of long-cloth (cutting down the stuff, not across), each four inches long and one inch and the sixteenth of an inch wide. These are to form shoulder straps, run and felled on at H and H in Fig. 37, having first just nipped off the corners with the scissors, as shown at J J in Fig. 38, treating both arm-holes alike. Then hem all round the arm-hole, and inside the shoulder-strap, making the hem no wider than the sixteenth of an inch, which is the smallest division you will find marked on an English yard-measure. (The French, who are much neater workers, preciser copyists, and better fitters, divide their inches into thirty parts.) Then hem the backs (K and K in Fig. 37) a quarter of an inch deep. Next hem all along the top, shoulder-straps included, a quarter of an inch deep, and run the narrowest tape in for a band. Cut two strips of long cloth (down the material) half an inch wide and nineteen inches long. Gather the waist of the body a little at each side of the back and in the centre of the front, as shown in Fig. 37, the limit of the gathers marked by four O's. Measure if the strips just cut exactly, and run it to the body on the wrong side, and turn it over. Join the other end of the band to the gathers of the skirt. The second band strip is used to line this, turning it down at both edges, and hemming it on the wrong side, taking care not to let the stitches show through on the right side. This completes the petticoat.

The first major event in any infant's life was the christening, although none would have been as lavish as that of their queen. The Cupola Room at Kensington Palace was prepared for Princess Victoria's christening on 24 June 1819. The room was filled with royalty and in the centre of it stood the great gold font. One of her godparents, the Prince Regent, was present and not in a good mood. As the child's names were called out one by one he shouted his objections to each. Finally instead of being baptized Georgiana Charlotte Augusta, the little Princess became Alexandrina (after her other godfather – the Czar of Russia) Victoria (after her mother, who sobbed quietly throughout the service).

Chaotic religious services were typical of the eighteenth-century way of life and in marked contrast to those of the

A charming illustration of a baby in its christening robe.

Victorian era. Such a traumatic christening would certainly not have fallen to the lot of one of the Princess's own subjects. They would have been baptized in church with a suitably well-behaved congregation and delighted parents and godparents. It was to be hoped that the baby would cry for, according to a mediaeval superstition that still had some currency in the nineteenth century, it was with a cry that the Devil was driven

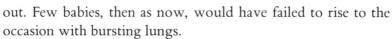

out. Few babies, then as now, would have failed to rise to the occasion with bursting lungs.

But before the church service there was the business of choosing names. In the eighteenth century and earlier most people were content to allow their children one name apiece. But with the growing affluence of the middle classes and an increasing tendency for them to imitate their royal betters, it became more and more fashionable to burden a child with a string of names – preferably with royal connections. Charles and Mary Lamb in their poem 'Choosing a Name' illustrated the problem neatly:

> I have got a new-born sister;
> I was nigh the first that kissed her.
> When the nursing woman brought her
> To papa, his infant daughter,
> How papa's dear eyes did glisten! –
> She will shortly be to christen:
> And papa has made the offer,
> I shall have the naming of her.
>
> Now I wonder what would please her,
> Charlotte, Julia or Louisa.
> Anne and Mary, they're too common;
> Joan's too formal for a woman;
> Jane's a prettier name beside;
> But we had a Jane that died.
> They would say, if 'twas Rebecca,
> That she was a little Quaker.
> Edith's pretty, but that looks
> Better in old English books;
> Ellen's left off long ago;
> Blanche is out of fashion now.
> None that I have named as yet
> Are so good as Margaret.
> Emily is neat and fine.

THE BABY.

What do you think of Caroline?
How I'm puzzled and perplexed
What to choose or think of next!
I am in a little fever.
Lest the name that I shall give her
Should disgrace her or defame her,
I will leave papa to name her.

Almost as crucial as the baby's names was his appearance on that all-important day. Christening robes were often religiously handed down from one child to another, but in the case of a first-born, it might well have been necessary to run one up for the occasion. The Victorian mother or nurse faced with the task would have been delighted to discover that it was not as difficult as she might have feared especially if, as several articles urged, the design and materials were kept as simple as possible:

> TO MAKE A CHRISTENING ROBE – take half a width of muslin and run tucks three and three with about four inches between each. Cut them apart. In paper cut the pattern of the front of the robe, which is to be a gore twenty-eight inches at the bottom, and ten inches at the top. Cut the half of it in paper, and allow three inches for the centre and outside insertion. Between every three tucks place a row of insertion, laying each on the paper pattern, so as to cut them the right length and not waste the embroidery which is expensive. Between every three tucks there must be a piece of inch wide embroidered insertion. Cut both tucks and insertion a little longer than the pattern to allow for working up, then neatly join them. Down the centre there is a row of embroidery, bordered each side by edging, and this is repeated at each side and carried round the bottom. A plain breadth of wide muslin completes the skirt, which is bordered all round by an embroidered flounce four inches deep. The body is composed of a stomacher of two tucks and one insertion, placed alternately.

An insertion double-edged, occupies the centre, and the braces, which form a berthe behind, are of the flouncing embroidery that robes the front of the skirt. The sleeves are plain, but covered with a frill of the flouncing. The waist and neck-band are made of insertion, and a narrow edge finishes the top. Christening robes for babes are sometimes made of lace instead of embroidery; but of course this requires everything *en suite* in richness and costliness, and is by no means necessary. Many parents prefer to use a plain robe for the christening.

After the church service with its dutifully bawling child and its few verses of 'In token that thou shalt not fear', the little party would make its way back to the family home, for it was the custom on such occasions for the mother to provide afternoon tea for the guests and godparents. The latter would be ready with some suitable present for the child – a small silver mug, a silver pencil or a coral teething ring all of which could be bought at shops such as Peter Robinson or Swears and Wells who specialized in christening gifts.

For the benefit of the newly-wed mother, a little book entitled *Party Giving on Every Scale* gave precise instructions on just how to arrange her tea party:

An afternoon tea party lasts at least three hours, and a guest should be served with as good a cup of tea or coffee on departure as on arrival. Tea that has been made for three hours acquires that peculiar stewy flavour; the especial property of tea served to travellers at most railway station 'Refreshment departments'. . . . As boiling milk is essential to coffee, so likewise is good cream essential to tea . . . In town the price of cream is 4/– per quart, and in the country 3/– per quart . . . Though claret-cup is invariably given at afternoon teas, it is less popular on these occasions than at lawn tennis and garden parties . . . Almond macaroons are much liked by ladies, as are

ratafias, cocoa-nut biscuits, chocolate-glacé biscuits, coffee biscuits, sponge biscuits; the cost of these are on the average 1/8– to 2/– per lb . . . Pound cake is also liked . . . cake should always be cut into small, short pieces, easy to hold in the fingers, as large slices of cake are awkward to hold, as well as too much to eat with a cup of tea . . . Many people, with whom economy is an object, do not indulge in fancy biscuits or rich cakes which run into shillings, if not into pounds, knowing also that a morsel of plain cake, or a slice of thin bread and butter, most commends itself to the generality of guests when drinking a cup of tea or coffee at an afternoon tea, and that when pretty and rich dainties are given they are a superfluity and an additional expense, and by no means a necessity.

With a sigh of relief as the last guest left, the Victorian couple would reflect that they were among the lucky ones. Their child, unlike so many in the nineteenth century, had survived the bath and bottle, the soaping and powdering, the ministrations of the monthly nurse and the stethoscope of the doctor, and was now safely christened. For a few months more he or she would be the property of the young mother until it was time for the first transition – one of which there would be little recognition – the transition from mother's to nurse's care, from first-floor bedroom to top-floor nursery:

BABY'S JOURNEY

Up, up the old oak staircase,
A journey to travel tonight;
The stars twinkle kindly above us,
And jewel the sky with their light.

Little head droops like a flower,
Pretty eyes can't open keep;
Baby knows nought of this journey, –
Baby has dropped off to sleep.

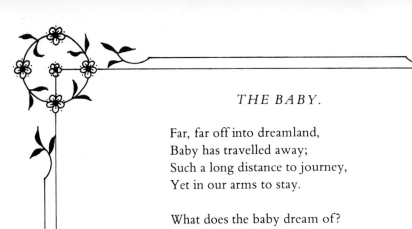

THE BABY.

Far, far off into dreamland,
Baby has travelled away;
Such a long distance to journey,
Yet in our arms to stay.

What does the baby dream of?
Does he go back once more
To the shining land of babies –
To that peaceful heaven-lit shore?

Does he just catch a glimpse of the angels,
And gaze in their radiant eyes?
I think, when he looks in our faces,
His own wears a look of the skies.

MRS SALE BARKER (*Little Wide-Awake,* 1890)

THE NURSERY.

THE Nursery is an indispensable apartment. It is the Children's Realm.

Our Homes and How to Beautify Them
H.J. JENNINGS (*c.* 1895)

ACCORDING to a mediaeval superstition, a baby had to be taken upstairs after birth if it was to rise in the world. If there were no stairs in the house, the mediaeval nurse would cheat the fates by climbing on to a chair holding the new arrival in her arms. In Victorian houses, such a perilous practice can seldom have been necessary as in most of them, the whole of the upper floor was given over to the children and the nursery staff. Behind a stout door and barred windows, the population of the nursery were at once safe and unheard.

As the century progressed, more and more interest was taken in the furnishing of the nursery. It became a room with a character all its own – perfectly adapted to the needs of its inhabitants and not just an extension of the box room:

> In the dreariness of town houses, nothing has struck me as so utterly cruel as the additional dreariness which generally pervades the rooms especially devoted to children – the nurseries of the house, the rooms in which our little ones spend so large a portion of their early lives – and yet I know of no rooms which should be made more cheerful and more beautiful in their general appearance than these. I do not mean that you are to put expensive cabinets, rare china or even pictures on the walls. These would not be understood, and would naturally help to the discomfort of the little inhabi-

tants, who would be told that they must not play or romp, for fear of damaging them in some way or other.

While the furniture should be strong and useful, it need not be prison-like; the walls need not be covered with some monotonous imitation tile paper, because it wears better than another.

In the windows of the day nursery there should be boxes of flowers, in which buttercups and daisies, primroses and daffodils, might be cultivated, to teach the little ones of the country, and of the nursery rhymes and fairy tales they love so well. A few shillings will buy bulbs or seeds enough to make a constant variety from springtide to winter, and an endless source of pleasure for little hands to tend and weave into fairy chains and tresses; and little eyes will brighten in watching for the outburst of some new flower. Let the walls be papered with some pleasant paper, in which the colours shall be bright and cheerful, distemper the upper portion of the room for health's sake, and varnish the paper if you please. But nowadays, when really good illustrations are generally and not as an exception to be found in so many of our monthly and weekly publications, why not, instead of destroying them, cut them out, or, better still, let the little ones do so, and paper them over the whole of the lower portion of the walls? A band of colour might be made by buying some of the Christmas books – which Mr H.S. Marks, R.A., Miss Kate Greenaway, and Mr Walter Crane have so charmingly and artistically illustrated – and by pasting the scenes in regular order and procession, as a kind of frieze under the upper band of distemper, varnished over to protect from dirt. The variously depicted scenes from the stories of Jack and the Bean Stalk, Cinderella and her sisters, of the numerous beautiful princesses and enchanted princes, and a host of other nursery rhymes and tales, may thus be used, while here and there, as varnished panels, might be pasted up the large Christmas coloured illustrations, which few Christmas numbers are now without. Why not cover the walls of the nurseries with illustrations, telling of the glories and, if you please, the horrors of war – teaching peace and goodwill by illustrating the antitype – of the various birds, beasts, and reptiles that went into the ark, of flowers, and all other things which are bright and beautiful? All these would make the children's room a bright and cheery spot, and in pleasant guise teach them many things, better than all the lesson books in the world.

There are some charming papers designed by Mr Walter Crane, illustrating some of the best-known nursery tales and rhymes, which are admirably adapted for the walls of day nurseries, and are cheap enough to be frequently changed. Do not have curtains of any sort in your nurseries; they only hold disease and dust. The more gay and cheerful your nurseries are, believe me, the brighter and happier will be your children. In the night nursery the walls should be all distempered, so as to be cleaned or redone at small cost at frequent intervals; for I am quite certain that here, above all things, it is essential to wash out, as often as possible, the peculiar bedroom atmosphere which must cling, in a measure, to the generally low rooms of the upper floor of a town house; a simple dark shade of colour will offer no spots or nightmare effects to drive away sleep or disturb the little ones in their times of feverish unrest or illness. But in the rooms they live in, there is no reason why the 'writing on the wall' should not be the earliest teaching of all that is beautiful in nature, art or science; and by the illustrations of fairy lore, incline the thoughts of our little ones to all that is graceful and beautiful in imaginative faculties. The knowledge thus gained, amid the smoke and dinginess of most of our large inland cities and towns, will tend to make the annual change to the country or seaside ten times more enjoyable, ten times more instructive.

The floors of the rooms should be stained and varnished or painted all over, and a small centre carpet pinned down in the

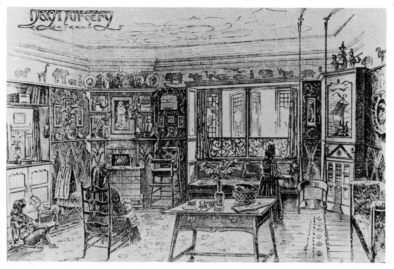

The day nursery – scheme as put forward by Mrs Panton in her book *The Gentlewoman's Home* (1890).

day nursery, so as to be easily taken up and cleaned; small strips of carpet or India matting laid down beside the beds will be amply sufficient in the night nursery. Let the beds be of iron, and the furniture strong and useful: painted or stained deal will be found amply sufficient, and is at the same time light and cheerful. London nurseries are, unfortunately, very low, and unless the back and front rooms communicate by large folding doors, which can be thrown open with the windows – so as to allow a thorough current of air to sweeten the rooms, when the children are out of them – there is much difficulty in securing good and proper ventilation. Too much care cannot be taken to obtain this, and large open gratings fixed over the doors and communicating with the staircase landing, with Boyles's ventilators in the chimneys, will be found good and effective means of obtaining a large amount of artificial ventilation. No pains should be spared to render the nurseries of the house as cheerful and pretty as possible, or to secure ample light and thorough ventilation.

THE NURSERY.

To surround our little ones with decoration and every-day objects, in which there shall be grace and beauty of design and colour, instead of the commonplace and vulgar tawdriness which in so many houses is thought good enough for the nurseries, will imbue them with a love and appreciative feeling for things of beauty and harmony of form and colour; but if we wish to have healthy children, we must have healthy homes, and, in studying how best to decorate the walls, do not let us forget that it is first of all imperative that there shall be no overcrowding of the generally low rooms, and that ample light and pure air are essential to their bodily and mental health and well-being.

Decoration and Furniture of Town Houses, R.W. EDIS (1881)

If only all Victorian nurseries had been as charming as that described by Mr Edis! Unfortunately they were not. In the earlier part of the century nurseries were too often merely attics into which was put discarded furniture that had ceased to be fashionable. Little effort was made to decorate them for their occupants and the very idea of window-boxes or suitable pictures would have seemed absurd to the average early nineteenth-century parent. Even Queen Victoria's nursery seems not to have been entirely designed for a young child. Lady Jane Ellice later recalled a visit she had made as a child to the royal nursery. The little Princess told her that she was not allowed to play on a white satin-covered sofa – hardly an ideal piece of furniture for a nursery and in stark contrast to the furnishing of the Queen's own children's nursery of later years. But unsuitable nurseries were not the sole preserve of royalty. Charlotte Yonge in her book *Chantry House* leaves a depressing picture of a nursery in the 1830s:

I hear of carpets, curtains, pictures in the existing nurseries. They must be palaces compared with our bare little attic where nothing was allowed that would gather dust. One bit of drugget by the fireplace where stood a round table at which the maids talked and darned stockings was all that hid the bare boards; the walls were plain as those of a workhouse, and when the London sun did shine, it glared into my eyes through the great unshaded windows. There was a deal table for the meals, and very plain meals they were, and two or three big presses painted white for our clothes, and one cupboard for our toys.

And in the 1840s the Lyttelton's family nursery was little better. Lucy Lyttelton, who later became Lady Cavendish, recalled in her *Memoires* that it was a large room filled with huge pieces of furniture – one big white cupboard for toys, a white wardrobe for clothes and a vast dark press containing crockery and food. A large round table and two bookcases completed the furnishings. But any child searching the bookshelves for some-

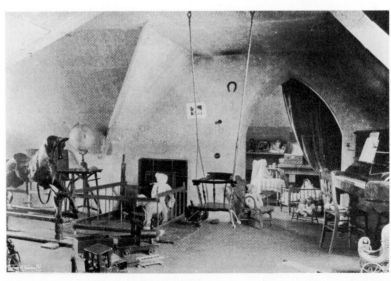

The attic nursery – a typical late Victorian nursery complete with piano, swinging chair and (later) teddy bears.

thing to read would have been bitterly disappointed. Apart from a few discarded adult volumes, the only contents were medical encyclopaedias. On the walls there were several prints of foreign men and women in national costume and a picture of the Queen and the Duchess of Kent. The austerity was only relieved by a brightly coloured map covered with pictures of birds, beasts and fishes.

However, as the century progressed the Victorians began to take more of an interest in the décor of the children's room – although few of them would have gone quite as far as H.J. Jennings, the author of *Our Homes and How to Beautify Them:*

> Happy are the people in that house wherein are heard 'the prattle of children's voices, the patter of tiny feet'. All the same, it is possible, no matter how sweet these sounds may be, to desire sometimes what Sydney Smith would have called 'a few brilliant flashes of silence'. The nursery is therefore an indispensable apartment. It is the children's realm, and it deserves a good deal more artistic consideration than is generally shown to it. I do not mean that it should be elaborately, or even expensively, decorated; that would be absurd. But neither, on the other hand, should it be turned into a gallery for the exhibition of glaring examples of cheap chromo-lithographic art. At an age when the mind is 'wax to receive and marble to retain', the child's pictorial surroundings are, as a rule, so far as taste is concerned, the reverse of educational. It starts life amidst an environment in which crude colour and chromatic discords are the prominent features. It imbibes an idea of art that is at once debasing and fallacious. When the child is older, it has to unlearn the prejudice in favour of vulgarity which this early tutelage has fostered. I contend that the nursery should be, if not a training in art, at least an object lesson in simplicity, refinement, and harmony of colour. It is possible to buy wallpapers which, while directly appealing to the interest of children by the pictorial narration of some

nursery tale, shall at the same time surround them with an artistic influence from the benefits of which they cannot possibly escape. I saw, not long since, a nursery, very simply but appropriately decorated. The dado was of match-boarding, painted an exceedingly pale terra cotta. Above this, the walls were distempered in a rich ivory white up to the frieze moulding. As for the frieze it was very deep, and consisted of scenes from 'Alice in Wonderland', beautifully copied from Sir John Tenniel's illustrations. The material was a plain pale buff canvas filling, the design being painted in colours. The bareness of the wall was relieved with quaint cupboards supported on corbels, and brackets holding amusing figures in wood of Swiss workmanship. On the floor was a warm-toned cork carpet.

All the furniture was of plain, simple, polished wood, without carving but finely shaped after old models, and upholstered in terra cotta leather. Here was a room severe enough in all conscience; yet it was beloved by the children; they were familiar with every character on the frieze; they knew every figure on the brackets; and they had a joyous sense of the beauty and quiet graciousness of their surroundings. It would be almost impossible for such children to grow up without an intuitive appreciation of tasteful effects.

A typical late nineteenth-century nursery is described by Alice Pollock in her autobiography, *Portrait of My Victorian Youth:*

We furnished the nursery with good plain furniture and the floor was covered with cork linoleum. There was an open coal fire, with a trivet on which stood the saucepan to heat the milk and barley water for the bottles. There was a high fender on wire mesh with a polished brass rail at the top, surrounding the fireplace. This was useful for airing the baby's clothes as well as preventing the children getting too near the fire. I made no attempt to get a grand bassinet but bought an untrimmed one and covered it myself with glazed chintz, mainly blue.

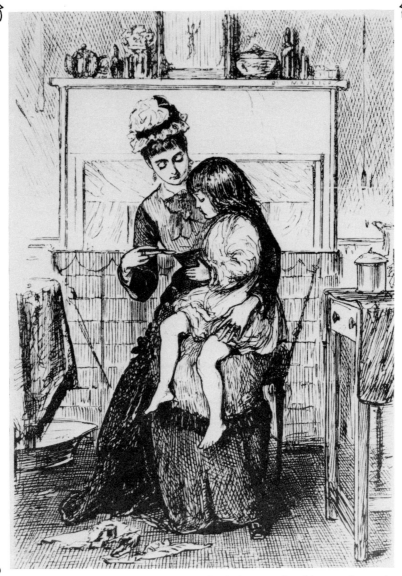

Supper-time – the nursery fire with its high fire-guard and brass rail was the focal point of so much nursery activity. Here the nurse is feeding a rather heavy child. The artist, du Maurier, has signed his name on the mantelpiece.

THE NURSERY.

Such simple and unpretentious nurseries must have been common enough at the turn of the century, but there were, in addition, much larger and grander establishments. A sizable Victorian house inhabited by a sizable family might well have boasted a complete nursery wing or the entire top floor of the house. There would then have been a day nursery, a night nursery and a schoolroom for the older children. In *Victoria-Bess* or *The Ups and Downs of a Doll's Life*, written by 'Brenda' in the 1880s, the doll is taken home from Cremer's toy shop by her new owner, Angela:

> By and by I was carried upstairs to a lofty and spacious nursery, over which I found Angela reigned supreme. She had no little brothers or sisters to share it with her. I was struck by its warmth and luxury, and with the toys I saw about in every direction, costly and numerous enough to have stocked Mr Cremer's shop pretty well.

And F. Gordon Roe, in his book, *The Victorian Child*, gives us a more detailed glimpse behind his nursery door:

> My nurseries were furnished with a variety of things, some especially bought, some seconded from other parts of the house. The result (though I was unaware of it) was a hotch-potch of new, of the merely old-fashioned, and of two or three items which would now pass muster as antique . . . Even my washstand was a mahogany affair which may well have been in use when the world was agog at the news of the Battle of Trafalgar. But my nursery table was of the ordinary kitchen kind, its wooden top left unstained for scouring, and my high chair was one of those late Victorian contraptions which could be folded to form a low seat with a playboard in front of it. It was solidly built was that chair and all too determinedly playful, with its coloured beads threaded on a rod from which they, provokingly, could not be removed, however much they rattled about.

THE NURSERY.

This high-chair was designed
by the eminent architect M.H. Baillie
Scott at the turn of the century.

Mechanical high-chair – at the touch of
a lever this ingeniously designed chair
becomes a child's rocking-chair.

Mr Roe's high chair was a typical piece of Victorian children's furniture. Although many nurseries throughout the nineteenth century were filled with adult furniture, there were nearly always several pieces especially designed for children either because of their diminutive size or because of their suitability for a child's needs. In an excellent book published at the beginning of Queen Victoria's reign, Mr Louden gave exhaustive advice even to those who wished to make their own nursery furniture:

> The first piece of furniture which an infant can be said to use is a bassinet, or portable bed. Fig. 1 is a bassinet two feet and a half long, the frame of which is made of wicker-work, with a hood which falls backwards or forwards as required. It is generally lined with printed material, or sometimes with dimity, to keep out the draught. The hood is covered with material, and two little curtains drop down from its front, which are looped up with tapes or ribands in the same manner as tent-bed material. A hair mattress stuffed very soft, and a small down pillow, complete the bed. The advantage of this bed is great; as the child, when asleep in it, is protected from currents of air from whatever direction they may come. The child may also be removed in it from one room to another without being disturbed. A mother will find such a bed particularly useful in the evening when the child is asleep beside her in the sitting-room; because it need not be disturbed, but may be carried in the bassinet to the bed-room, and there placed by the side of the bed; whereas, if the child were asleep on a sofa, its removal, by taking it up in the arms, would be certain to awake it, and the mother might lose her rest for several hours.
>
> Cribs are bedsteads for children so young as to render it unsafe to trust them by themselves in beds with unguarded sides. They are generally intended to be placed, during the night, by the bedside of the mother; and for that purpose, the height of the crib should correspond with that of the large bed,

THE NURSERY.

Fig. 1

Fig. 2

and one of its sides be made to lift out. This is effected by grooves in the upright posts, with tongues on the end styles of the side. Fig. 2 is a design for a crib in the Grecian style, and Fig. 3 for one in the Gothic style, both by Mr Dalziel, who recommends that the heads of the bed-screws, with which Fig. 2 is screwed together, should be concealed by a wooden cap instead of by a brass one, as is commonly done. In the leg of the Gothic crib, the screw is concealed by means of a small wooden panel made to be taken out. The turned rails of the sides, in Fig. 2, and the plain rails in the Gothic design, are considered better than the open canework usually employed for crib sides, through which children are apt to put their fingers and hurt themselves. Cribs are sometimes made with only one side, the rail on that opposite being held close to the rail of the large bed by hooks and eyes. Any joiner might make these cribs of deal, or any other cheap wood; and they may be painted or stained to harmonize with the bedstead and chairs of the room in which they are to be placed. Fig. 4 is a view of a cheap crib, the frame and bottom of which are formed of wrought iron, and the sides and ends of deal. It may be made for fifteen shillings. Swinging cribs and cradles are now justly exploded.

Bedding includes palliasses, or straw mattresses; hair, wool, or other mattresses; hay, chaff, or feather beds; bolsters, pillows, sheets, blankets, and counterpanes. The palliass is an inflexible mattress, stuffed with drawn wheat straw; placed as the lower layer of the bedding, for the purpose of raising it, and giving a more agreeable basis to the feather-bed. The common mattress is formed by stuffing a canvas case with flocks, wool, baked horse-hair, sea grass, technically called *Ulva marina*, or any other articles which when put together form an elastic body, and afterwards quilting it down, and covering it with a description of cloth called ticken. The feather-bed and the pillows are stuffed with feathers. In Scotland, mattressses and bolsters, exceedingly agreeable to

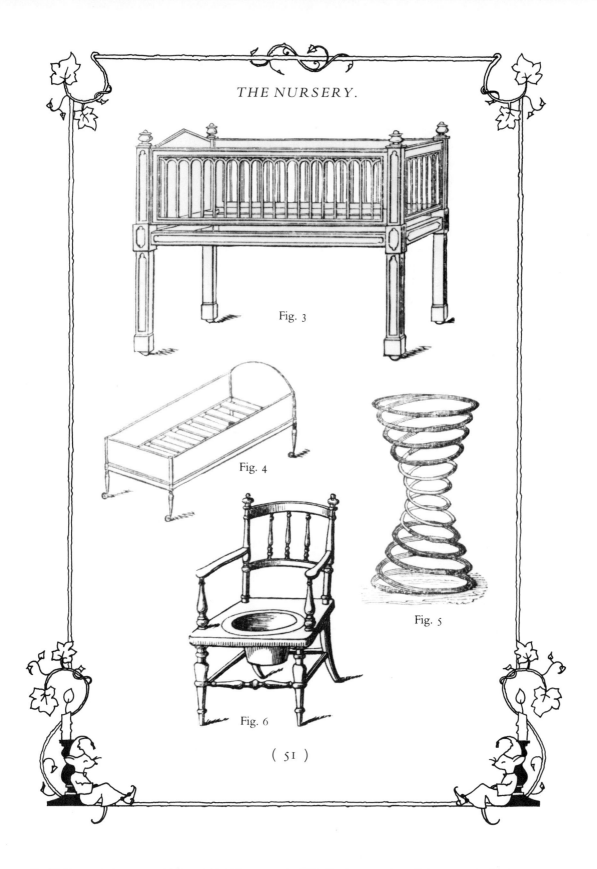

THE NURSERY.

Fig. 3

Fig. 4

Fig. 5

Fig. 6

sleep upon, are stuffed with the outer chaff of the oat, carefully sifted from the smaller chaff, and from all dust, and renewed once a year. In Italy, and in countries where the maize is in common culture, excellent mattresses are formed by stuffing them with the chaff of that grain. A few flowers of the hop mixed with the chaff of the bolster give that article an agreeable fragrance, which is at the same time soporific. George III at one time slept on a pillow entirely stuffed with hops; and some years ago, when in Worcestershire, we think in 1815, we slept at a farmhouse, on a bed, bolster, and pillows, all stuffed with hops, and found that they formed a species of bedding soft and powerfully fragrant, though said to be unwholesome.

Substitutes for stuffing to beds, bolsters and pillows have been proposed by upholsterers at different times, and some of them have been lately a good deal used; of these we shall mention three; viz., wire springs, air and water.

Wires springs for stuffing are nothing more than spiral coils of wire, Fig. 5, generally an eighth of an inch in diameter for mattresses, and smaller for cushions, carriage seats, &c. These springs are placed, side by side, on interlaced webbing, strained to a frame of the size of the intended bed, cushion or seat; they are then confined by cords to one height, and covered by a piece of ticken or strong canvas, strained tightly over them. On this is spread a layer of curled horse-hair, and an upper cover of ticken is then placed over the whole, and nailed down tight to the underside of the wooden frame with tacks. For our own part, we prefer beds made with these spiral springs to any other; not only from their greater elasticity, and the equal diffusion of the support which they afford to the body, but because, from the quantity of air among the springs, they can never become so warm as beds stuffed with any of the ordinary materials. The effect of spiral springs as stuffing has been long known to men of science; but so little to upholsterers, that a patent for using them in stuffing was taken out, some years ago, as a new invention. Beds and seats of this description are now, however, made by upholsterers generally, and the springs may be had from Birmingham by the hundred weight.

Chairs are the next articles made use of by children; and those about London are of four kinds. Fig. 6 is a child's chair of the first kind, having a night pan, and a matted seat. A small stuffed flannel of the size of the seat, and having a round hole in the centre, is generally placed over it when it is to be used, in order to prevent the pan from hurting the child. (In some districts of Italy, and other parts of the Continent, rings of stuffed cloth, or stuffed leather, or of rush matting, are used for the same purpose by grown-up persons.) In England, infants of ordinary health and strength are put into chairs of this kind, when between three and four months old . . .

Fig. 7 is a child's washing-stand, consisting of a table about eighteen inches high, with a large basin and a soap cup sunk in one side of the top. The table is made lower than a chair, in order that the nurse may have the more power over the child when she is washing it. When the child is only a few weeks old, it is immersed, or bathed in the basin; but as it grows larger, it sits on the top of the table, with its legs in the water.

To enable the mother who has no servants, to relieve herself at pleasure from carrying her child, there are various contrivances in use in England, which deserve to be mentioned; and there is one, for cleanliness and decency, which deserves imitation in every country, and more especially in our own. Fig. 8 is a swing chair, formed out of ten pieces of elder tree (a), six inches long, and an inch and a half in diameter, with the pith burnt out with a redhot poker, or other iron; nine rails (b), about a foot long with a round hole at each extremity; a bottom board (c), a foot square, with a round hole in each corner and four sash lines or cords about a quarter of an inch in diameter, and of sufficient length to reach from the ceiling of the room in which the chair is to be hung. Knots being made on the ends of the lines, the tubes and rails are strung on as in

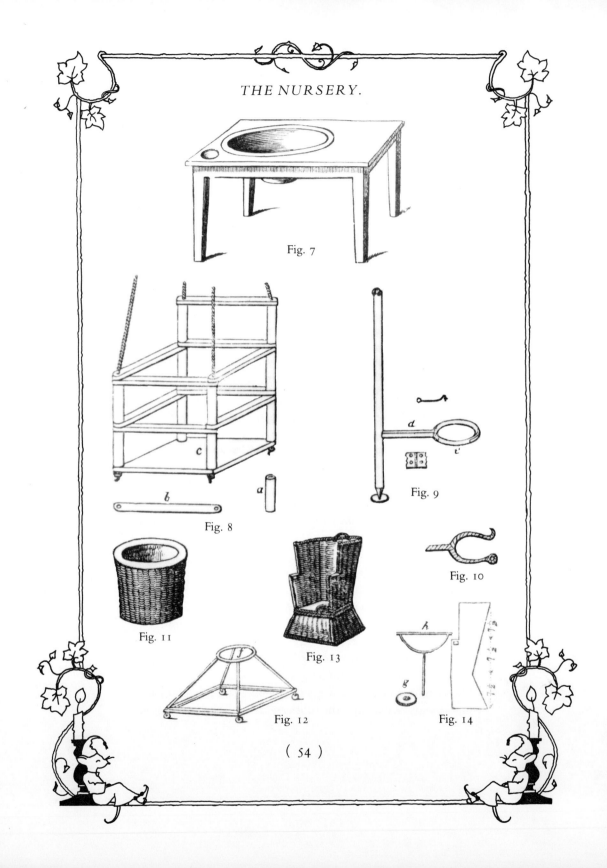

Fig. 7

Fig. 8

Fig. 9

Fig. 10

Fig. 11

Fig. 12

Fig. 13

Fig. 14

the figure, and the other ends of the cords tied together and suspended from a hook in the ceiling. By omitting four of the cylinders, and four of the rails, a chair may be made for an infant of the earliest age. A cushion may be put in the bottom, or the bottom may be stuffed.

Fig. 9 is a *go-gin* for a child who can stand, to teach him to walk. It consists of a perpendicular shaft, long enough to reach from the floor to the ceiling, which turns in a hole in a brick or stone of the floor and within a staple driven into the side of one of the ceiling joists, or by any similar means. The piece (d), about eighteen inches long, is mortised into the upright shaft, about eighteen inches from the ground; and the wooden ring, (e), about seven or eight inches in diameter, has a piece about six inches long, which is hinged at one end, and fastened with a hook and eye at the other. This opens, and the child being put in is enclosed at the height of the waist. The ring taking part of the child's weight, he cannot fall, and he soon learns to walk. Frequently this ring is made of twisted withy, (Fig. 10), with an eye at one extremity and a hook at the other: or each extremity is made to terminate in a loop, and when the child is put into the ring one of these is slipped over the other, and a hooked wooden pin serves to keep them together: in both cases the hinge is made like that of the handle of a basket. Both these pieces of furniture are made in England by every cottager for himself. Fig. 11 is a hollow cylinder, nothing more than the section of the trunk of an old pollard tree, commonly to be met with in England, the inside and the upper edge are smoothed, and a child just able to stand is put into it, while its mother is at work by its side, or going about the business of the house. Fig. 12 is a *go-cart* which is frequently made of willow rods without castors, but is here shown as a piece of carpentry, standing on castors. The ring (f) at the top, opens with a hinge, and shuts. Children readily learn to walk by these machines, without the danger of falling. Fig. 13 is a pierced chair, made entirely of wickerwork, which costs,

complete, about London, only four shillings and sixpence, while there is a cheaper sort, with a rush bottom at two shillings and sixpence. Everyone who can make a basket can make a chair of this description. First form the skeleton frame (Fig. 14); then commence round the circular hole in the centre, and work in either willow rods or rushes towards the extremities, according to the kind of chair it may be wished to produce. The cover of the vase in the seat (g) is lifted off by two thumb holes, so as to be quite flat for the child to sit upon when the vase is not in use. There are two holes in the elbows of the chair through which may be placed either simply a rod to keep the child from falling out, or a table flap (h), with two pins at the ends to fit into the holes; the table being also supported by a movable leg in front, and having a ledge round it for holding the child's playthings; its pins being kept in their holes by the elasticity of the sides of the chair. In England the cottager's child is placed on a chair of this sort after he is a week old; but in Scotland there is neither this chair, nor any substitute for it. In both countries there are small chairs with long feet, for elevating children to the height of an ordinary table, so that they may sit and eat with their parents; and these, like the pierced chair, ought to be universally in use.

Cribs, chairs and go-gins apart, probably the most indispensable single piece of equipment in or out of the Victorian nursery was the perambulator. This was the invention of a certain Charles Burton who, while in America, had been struck by the fact that:

> Carrying a heavy child in the arms – when this is done by young and growing girls, such as nursemaids most frequently are – is not only a wearisome occupation, but often one which, through inducing diseases of the spine, is the cause of serious injuries, the effects of which may last through life.

Having produced his first perambulator in America in 1848,

The perambulator was an invention of the 1840s.
This type, which became known as the 'Victoria', was exhibited at the
Great Exhibition in 1851.

Burton returned to England, exhibited his invention at the Great
Exhibition in 1851 and took out a patent for it. The idea
immediately caught the public imagination and demand for the
new perambulators was enormous. Burton moved from his
small shop in Kensington to more spacious premises in Oxford
Street and before his death he was running shops there, in Regent
Street and in Piccadilly. But throughout the nineteenth century
Oxford Street remained the centre of the baby carriage trade.

The most usual design for an early Victorian perambulator
was the three-wheeled push-chair in which the child faces in the
direction he is being pushed. But other designs proliferated, as
did new patent methods of springing and weather-proofing. The
careful Victorian made sure he asked for advice before investing
in what might appear better than it was:

An unlikely scene – a father takes his daughter for a walk in a miniature perambulator of the 'Victoria' type.

In a well-made perambulator, the body is, on account of its lightness and toughness, made entirely of birchwood. The splashboard and wings, which are essential as preventing injury to the child's clothing in muddy weather, are best formed of solid leather; American cloth, which is a cheap imitation of that material, looks and wears well for a time, and is far less expensive, but is, of course, inferior in point of durability. The frame, wheels, and handles, are of malleable iron, and the springs of good steel, while that part of the handle which is intended to be grasped may be made either of fancy wood or of what is now more fashionable, opal glass. The inside is stuffed and cushioned in the same manner as any other carriage, and the hoods, which are absolutely necessary to the comfort of the occupant, are of two kinds. In one they are made like that of an ordinary barouche; metal ribs – with a covering of leather, coburg, alpaca, or holland – cross the perambulator, and are so constructed as to admit of their folding backwards, and fastened by screws at the sides in such a manner as to allow of the whole hood being removed at pleasure. Upon this the second description – the patent canopy – is an improvement, being less weighty and cumbersome, and more elegant in appearance. A curved rod of iron, fitting into a socket at the back of the perambulator, supports a species of parasol, which when opened completely protects the occupant, and when closed can be covered with a case, and thus secured from dust. The principle of this sunshade differs from that of the ordinary parasol or umbrella, in its opening laterally instead of vertically. . . . An invention obviating jolting in the passage over rough stones or other inequalities, is the spiral spring, introduced in the perambulators made by Mr Morley of 487, New Oxford Street. The peculiar construction of this reduces the effect of any uneven motion to the minimum . . .

When a perambulator for two children is bought, it will be well to see that it has a division in the centre to secure to each

For summer walks – a charming basket-work
perambulator sold by Hitching of London.

Nursery accessories – an advertisement for perambulators and high-chairs from
Farmer, Lane and Co., *c.*1890.

child its proper proportion of room. If the carriage have a hood, one with joints is to be chosen in preference since the incomplete arrangement of a strap in front to keep the hood extended is liable, being constantly looked at by the child, to render it cross-eyed. Another desirable point in a hooded perambulator is a glass light in the back, through which the child may be constantly watched by its nurse; without this she can only see that it retains its proper position – and that it is right in every other respect – by leaving the handle and coming to the front, which she will not be likely to do too often.

When the additional expense is not an object, real morocco makes by far the most handsome and enduring lining, and should be chosen. There should be a good and brilliant surface to the painted portions, as this will indicate the proper thickness and consequent durability of the paint, five coats being considered necessary to give such a surface; and we may in this place remark that the paint, and even the body of the carriage itself, may be made much more enduring by simply being varnished once a year.

Cassell's Household Guide

Additional requirements of the suitable perambulator were that it should be provided with a stout apron to cover the body of the occupant and that, if possible, the handles and other protrusions should be removable. With all these qualifications, a good perambulator could last several years and even several generations, as the present authors know.

In the 1880s the 'baby-carriage' appeared. This was a perambulator in which a child could lie down and was therefore suitable for younger children. Designs proliferated throughout the later years of the last century, but it was the classic early perambulator that caught the imagination of Mrs Adams Acton. In *The Adventures of a Perambulator* she traced the journey of a

The baby carriage – a later development of the perambulator in which younger children could lie down. This one is fitted with a patent brake.

DUNKLEY'S,
BIRMINGHAM.

PATENT

FAST

CUSHION

TYRES.

Patent Suspension **Perambucot.**   Patent Reversible Mail Cart.

LONDON DEPÔT: {1

76, HOUNDSDITCH.

Pushed and pulled – transport novelties for children: Dunkley's Perambucot and Patent Reversible Mail Cart.

(62)

very untypical Victorian family. One summer's day in 1890, Papa, Mamma, Claud, Sissy, Robin, Atom (a dog), Scrap (another), Sunbeam (the baby), Mollins (the nurse) and Ada (the maid) all set out to walk from London to Scotland – all, that is, except Sunbeam who travelled in the perambulator. But before they could set out, the perambulator had to be serviced:

> Out it came into the garden – it still looked fresh and smart from that visit to Whiteley's before the last fire, but one or two brass-headed screws and buttons were wanting. 'Take it round to the ironmongers tomorrow, Mollins, and see that everything is right and in good order; and oil all the wheels and things well with paraffin oil – see that the apron and hood are well brushed up.' 'The perambulator shall be alright,' remarked Mollins, with a sparkle in her eyes, and a flush on her cheeks.

After a series of breathtaking adventures, including losing the perambulator on a train to Beith, the family reach their destination and eventually arrive home to be heralded by incredulous Londoners:

> Very much to the surprise of the whole party, they found they had achieved a considerable notoriety . . . Mamma was interviewed by reporters, who copied one another's reports all over the country, with any additions or remarks which suited their fancies . . . Mollins never went out without being stopped, if she had the perambulator; and visitors enquired if she would excuse them asking, but *was* that 'the perambulator', and *were* those the children who had walked to Scotland?
>
> And Mollins, with pride, owned that all were the real articles, herself into the bargain . . .

THE NURSE.

WHEN the voices of children are heard on the green,
And laughing is heard on the hill,
My heart is at rest within my breast,
And everything else is still.

'Nurse's Song', WILLIAM BLAKE

MOLLINS, the nurse in *The Adventures of a Perambulator*, is the
stuff of which all good Victorian nurses are made. Much play is
made of the fact that she is forgetful – one day she leaves her
holdall behind in Hendon and has to go back for it – but in all
other respects she is the perfect nanny, being responsible, truthful
and endearingly enthusiastic in the face of often excruciating
discomfort.

Few young mothers in the nineteenth century could hope to
find a Mollins to take charge of their nurseries. In a relentless
search for the perfect applicant they would undoubtedly have
interviewed many women as well as consulting some of the
contemporary journals offering advice as to the essential qualifications for the position:

> Next to the engagement of a governess, that of a nurse
> requires the greatest consideration. If the mother of the child-
> ren spends a great deal of time in the nursery, she is naturally
> the individual to whom the little ones look for advice and
> assistance. But if from pressure of business, ill-health or any
> other cause, she is compelled to confide the care of her
> offspring to a stranger, too much care cannot be taken to
> secure the services of a well-informed, kind-hearted deputy.
> The most essential qualities to seek in a nursery attendant are
> truthfulness, intelligence, cheerfulness and cleanliness. As a

THE NURSE.

The afternoon walk – 'Whenever the plan of the day's work rests with the nurse, the primary consideration should be to secure plenty of time for out-door recreation and exercise.'

general rule, these qualities are not very generally to be found in the class of domestic servants from which inferior situations in a household are filled. Nurses, as representatives of mothers, should be drawn from the more highly educated circles of society than usually constitute the domestic servant class. Daughters of small tradesmen, ill-paid civil service employees, and clerks, that have enjoyed the training which a well-regulated home above the reach of actual want affords, are excellent, generally speaking, as upper nurses; and the assistance of such, when once secured, should be rewarded in a generous spirit.

And how should the nurse be dressed?

Steel hoops should never be worn in the nursery, however much the foolish fashion may be adhered to out of doors. Neither should long skirts be worn, tripping little children up

as they are liable to do. Gowns made of washable materials are most suitable. These are easily cleansed if soiled by nursery duties, and cost but little to renew. A waterproof apron worn under the ordinary white apron will be found a great comfort to a nurse, and might be supplied with advantage at the cost of an employer. Every nurse should also be furnished with a long, loose, warm wrapper, made like a dressing-gown, for night wear, when her duties require her to rise from her bed to take a baby to and from the mother's room. This garment should be purchased by the mistress of the house, and kept for the use of any nurse who many succeed to the situation.

Throughout nineteenth-century literature there are references to 'disagreements' among the members of staff – blood-feuds and battles royal behind the green baize doors. One member of the staff, however, who seemed constantly to be above such bickerings was the nurse. In her fastness on the upper floor she commanded a small nursery staff of her own and was seldom involved in imbroglios below stairs. The reason for this state of affairs becomes much clearer after reading the above extract. The nurse was drawn from a different class of society to the other servants – she was, perhaps, the daughter of an 'ill-paid' civil servant who had been brought up in a household 'above the reach of actual want'. Her sister chamber-maid – from the working classes – would never have aspired to a nurse's position. She was deemed to have filled at one time or another almost every situation in ever-varying households, and her comparatively nomadic existence was calculated to mingle her experience with 'bitterness and dissatisfaction'. Some of that bitterness would have undoubtedly been caused by contemplation of the nurse's lot – better-fed and better-paid than herself and held in infinitely higher regard by her employers.

In larger establishments, however, the chamber-maid might have aspired to the dizzy heights of nursery-maid. Although she

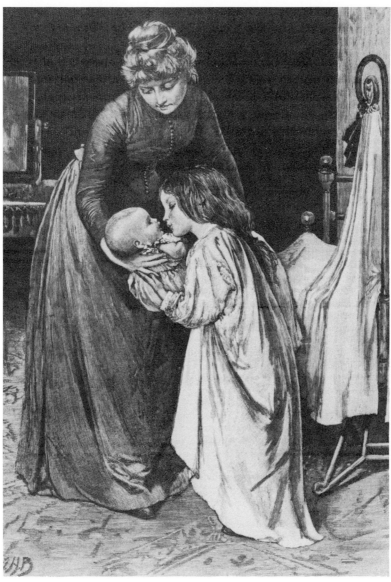

A morning visit – Victorian children, like all children, took a great interest in their baby brothers and sisters. A good nurse encouraged this interest.

THE NURSE.

The Indian connection – a Victorian boy with his Aya. In the second half of the nineteenth century families who had been in India often brought their native nurses back to England.

THE NURSE.

On the nurse's day off, the nurse-maid is proud to be left
in charge of the baby.

(69)

The Victorian boy, home from school for the holidays, delights in disrupting
the ordered calm of the nursery.

would have been under the direct rule of the nurse, she would
certainly have had a cosier life if not an easier one. Here again
qualifications were high:

> In choosing a nursery-maid, early-rising, good-temper, and
> strength of constitution are necessary qualifications. If a
> nursery-maid has time to spare from more active duties, it is
> advisable that she should be a fair needle-woman; not only
> that she may assist in mending the children's clothes, but
> because a young person who has a taste for sewing is generally
> more companionable to the little folks in the nursery than one
> who has no inducement to sit down when her more active
> duties are finished.
>
> In addition to the ordinary duties of the nursery, a nurse-
> maid is generally required to assist in washing infants' linen,
> flannels, socks, frills, tuckers, etc. Time should be allowed for
> this work on a certain day of the week; the children, mean-

while, being placed entirely under the care of the nurse or the mother.

The Victorian nurse-maid was also responsible for all the menial tasks in the nursery – cleaning the grate, lighting the fire, cleaning the rooms, fetching the meals and generally seeing to the wants of the nurse and her small charges – as well as taking the children for their afternoon walk. There can have been very little spare time for mending the children's clothes. However, there was always a small chance that one day she would be able to apply for a position as a nurse, although she would find the competition very hot.

Throughout the nineteenth century, the newspapers and periodicals abounded with advertisements for nurses. It is some measure of the esteem in which such servants were held that their

Victorian parents would 'receive' their children for an hour or so after tea and before they changed for dinner. Usually, the nurse would also be in attendance at this time.

THE NURSE.

advertisements always appeared at the head of the 'domestic appointments' columns. There, under the headings: 'Head Nurses', 'Upper Nurses', 'Nurses', 'Under Nurses' and 'Nurse-maids' they applied in their hundreds for jobs. Some even saw such employment as a way to pay their passages abroad:

> A well-educated passenger, going out to India by P. & O. Company's ship end of August or beginning of October, would be glad to assist a lady passenger with one or two children for part passage-money, or would take sole charge for £30 . . .
> Address:– Mrs D. care of Mrs Bryant, 15 Battison Street, Bedford.

> *The Lady*, 7 July 1887

Heard and not seen – many Victorian mothers, used to a nurse's ministrations, were quite incapable of coping with their own children.

(72)

Children in the nineteenth century were bathed in a tin bath in front of the nursery fire. In this advertisement from the 1890s, the child's mother has joined the nurse for the occasion.

THE NURSE.

Mrs D. was quite possibly unmarried. But her position as a nurse in a well-to-do household allowed her the courtesy title 'Mrs' – a privilege she shared with the cook.

Having found the ideal nurse and nursemaid, the Victorian mother would have been at pains to acquaint them with the routine that she expected them to follow. The correct organization of the day was vital to the smooth running of the nursery as contemporary manuals were quick to point out:

> Whenever the plan of the day's work rests with the nurse, the primary consideration should be to secure plenty of time for out-door exercise and recreation. With this view, nursery cleansing, and other arrangements should be made subservient to the state of the weather, in order that exercise in the open air may be taken in the finest part of the day. As young children usually wake early, the morning walk should, in summer time, take place before the sun's heat is oppressive. The most healthy time for walking out in the summer months is between eight and ten o'clock in the morning, and from half-past five till seven o'clock in the evening. In the spring and fall of the year, from ten to twelve o'clock in the morning, and from three till five o'clock in the afternoon, will be found equally suitable. Young children should never be exposed to the burning heat of the sun, neither should they be allowed to sit down in the parks and squares of towns. As far as it is possible, little children residing in the country should spend the greater part of their time out of doors; the nurse, if necessary, doing any light needlework in the meantime. Any kind of game which exercises the limbs of children whilst in the open air, is conducive to health; only when passing through the streets should they be required to walk hand in hand.

While the children and their nurse were out walking the nurse-maid was kept busy. Her duties at such times were to open

The shower-bath – the Pooteresque father introduces the household to a new invention to the dismay of the staff and the horror of his children.

the windows to air the rooms, to air the bedding, to scrub the nursery floor and to light the fire. When they returned, the children were encouraged to rest:

> All children under four years of age (and as much later as the habit can be enforced) should be persuaded to rest on returning home from a walk – the little ones to sleep, and the older ones to read books or look at pictures, whilst in a recumbent position.
>
> In the meanwhile, the nurse should wash and dress herself thoroughly in another room, if she has been prevented from doing so in the earlier part of the morning. Whilst the children are taking their morning nap is the best time for the nurse to do any little work not suitable to the nursery. Before leaving the room, however, she should take every precaution to prevent accidents, by the children falling out of bed, playing with the fire, or what not.

THE NURSE.

In order to leave no inducement to the children to lie awake in their beds, the nursery blinds should be drawn down during the morning hour of slumber. All toys should be put out of sight, and the apartment made to appear as little suggestive of play as possible. In the waking hours of children the reverse should be the case. The more the floor is bestrewn with toys, and the more nursery litter is about, the more happy the place is to its infant denizens. A skilful nurse will know when to enforce habits of order, and when to give way to a natural inclination on the part of children to create confusion.

Sadly the nursery 'bestrewn with toys' was not typical of all Victorian nurseries. No more was Mollins with her sweet disposition typical of all Victorian nurses. The nineteenth century had its share of nursery tyrants like Eleanor and Harry Farjeon's nurse, Julia:

Harry had been too much confined upstairs with Julia. They thought that all was well. Whenever he climbed downstairs to them, he came down singing 'The Old Armchair':
  'How vey tittered! how vey roared!'
His quavering little voice chanted all the way.
  'How happy the child sounds', smiled Ben and Maggie; and when the happy child ran in crying, 'I-do-love-Julia-I do!' they smiled again.
  One night when Julia was out, and Mama was giving Harry his bath, she noticed his skinny little arm was black and blue.
  'Why, Harry, what's this?'
The child looked at her with his dark, solemn eyes.
  'Julia did it.'
Mama feels sick.
  'When did she do it, Harry?'
  'When I come downstairs. Julia says sing-ve-ol'-Armchair an' pinches me ee-eee!'
The little features are suddenly contorted.

‘Ear-corset’ – an extraordinary piece of patent headgear showing
that it was not only Victorian waists that were kept in.

THE NURSE.

'Harry,' asks Mama, 'Who tells you to say I-do-love-Julia?'
'Julia does,' says Harry.

A Nursery in the Nineties, ELEANOR FARJEON

Lord Curzon also remembered his own cruel nurse:

> In her savage moments she was a brutal and vindictive tyrant;
> and I have often thought since that she must have been insane.
> She persecuted and beat us in the most cruel way and estab-
> lished over us a system of terrorism so complete that not one
> of us ever mustered up the courage to walk upstairs to tell our
> father or mother. She spanked us with the sole of her slipper
> on the bare back, beat us with her brushes, tied us up for long
> hours to chairs in uncomfortable positions with our hands
> holding a pole or a blackboard behind our backs, shut us up in
> darkness . . . I suppose no children well-born and well-placed
> ever cried so much or so justly.

The problem was that so often the nurse was a complete
autocrat in her own nursery. The children, as far as some
Victorian parents were concerned, were seldom seen and never
heard – out of sight if not totally out of mind. As long as the
status quo was maintained and the nursery and adult worlds
appeared to run smoothly and independently, nobody – even the
parents – asked questions that really ought to have been asked.
For so many Victorian children their only contact with their
parents was that celebrated hour after tea in the drawing room,
and even then nurse was usually in attendance, to receive plaudits
on the exemplary behaviour and appearance of her charges. A
nursery revolution was unthinkable to most children and for
every cruel nurse who was exposed there must have been
hundreds whose misdeeds were never discovered. In addition,
the tremendous weight that Victorians put upon discipline in the
bringing up of children gave rise to some treatments that seem
barbaric to us today. The line between cruelty and what passed
for diligence in a nurse must have been a fine one.

(78)

However, the particularly Victorian puritan ethic that the nastier a thing was the better it was for one, was not by any means universal in nineteenth-century England. Discipline, it is true, was considered important but discipline was, in most cases, tempered with benevolence.

The goodnight kiss.

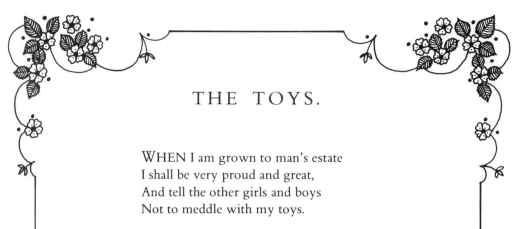

THE TOYS.

WHEN I am grown to man's estate
I shall be very proud and great,
And tell the other girls and boys
Not to meddle with my toys.

ROBERT LOUIS STEVENSON

TO OPEN the toy cupboard in a Victorian nursery was to risk being bowled over by an avalanche of childish objects of every shape and hue. Only the larger toys like the rocking horse and dolls' house were left out at night. The rest were crammed in more or less tidily to await the dawn of another day's play.

Among the toys for younger children were the soft toys. These appeared in nurseries only at the end of the nineteenth century – apart, that is, from the rag doll which is of far earlier origin. But the late-Victorian child could well have cuddled a toy lamb, a duck, a small pony or, best of all perhaps, a golliwog. Florence and Bertha Upton's golliwogg (spelt with two g's) stories first appeared in 1895 and caused an immediate furore. Golliwogs became all the rage and there can have been few Victorian nurseries without at least one. Teddy bears did not appear until 1902 when Theodore Roosevelt baulked at shooting a bear cub in the Rockies and, by way of a cartoon portraying the incident in the *Washington Evening Star*, began a new craze and a new industry in toys. But the Victorian nursery was bereft of bears.

Perennial favourites such as hoops and sticks, tops, balls and marbles were also much to the fore in the toy cupboard, as were much more intricate mechanical toys made by the master toy-makers of Bavaria. For girls, of course, there were dolls; dolls to

"LE MAGASIN DES ENFANTS"

Hamley's Toys

TOYS.

DOLLS.

GAMES.

The Latest Continental Novelties.

Great Assortment from 6d. upwards.

ILLUSTRATED CATALOGUE POST FREE.

HAMLEY, Bros.

THE COURT TOYMEN,

64, REGENT STREET,

LONDON, W.

Hamleys were among the many Victorian toy shops who spent a great deal of money on advertising. None of the others, however, could add the prestigious phrase 'The Court Toymen' after their names.

be dressed for every occasion; baby dolls and almost grown-up dolls as well as dolls small enough to live in the dolls' house. For boys there were lead soldiers in whole armies, as well as castles

Clockwork toys – a by-product of the Swiss watchmaking industry – became cheaper and more widespread as the century progressed. This toy rabbit arises from the heart of the lettuce.

for them to defend. One Victorian educationalist heartily approved of dolls, but frowned on soldiers:

> Girls possess a desire for nursing dolls; it arises from an original propensity of the mind – the love of children. Provide dolls, therefore, for infant girls. Besides amusing them, the making and putting off and on of dolls' clothes, teaches lessons of neatness, and cultivates sentiments of affection.
>
> Whilst on this subject, it may be proper to caution parents against giving their children toys of a kind likely to encourage warlike or savage propensities; such as mimic guns, swords or other military accoutrements. We have remarked that toys of this kind are commonly given to children in France, a practice which perhaps tends to nourish a love of war in our neighbours. We hope English parents will avoid this folly, and impart toys only of a simply amusing or improving tendency.
>
> 'The Management of Infants', Chambers Miscellany of Useful and Entertaining Tracts

One has only to see the life-sized toy fort and its accoutrements at Osborne House to realize that neither the Queen, Prince Albert nor the royal princes would have taken such advice very much to heart. However, very close to the fort is something of which the writer would have greatly approved. Prince Albert was keen that his children should learn from an early age that there is dignity in labour. He therefore marked out individual gardens for each and had miniature garden tools made with which the royal princes and princesses cultivated their plots. Taken together with the miniature kitchens in the Swiss chalet, complete with every utensil especially made, the royal collection of improving toys at Osborne must be unrivalled in history. The educational aspect of toys was something that all Victorian writers warmed to:

> Playing with toys may be said to be not only an amusement,

The rocking horse – the pride of any nursery. This late nineteenth-century model even has seats for passengers.

but the proper occupation of children. Let them, therefore, have what toys you can afford to purchase. Such things as a box of wooden bricks, wherewith to build houses, or a slate and pencil, are inexhaustible sources of recreation. Books of prints of birds, or animals in general, may be employed with great advantage, because they excite questions, afford the parent opportunities of giving much valuable oral instruction, and induce that love of enquiry, which is the parent of knowledge.   ibid.

And even when a toy was not intrinsically educational, a story about it could well be. Angela's doll, Victoria-Bess, whose impression of her owner's nursery was so favourable, turns out in the story to be as empty-headed and as vain as her new owner. When Angela's poor cousin Katie comes to tea she brings her doll – Mignonette, a cheap rag one in marked contrast to the much grander Victoria-Bess. The dolls are introduced to each other . . .

'Oh, a *rag* doll!' said Angela. 'Do you like rag dolls? Do you think they are nice?'

'I don't think they're so pretty as wax,' replied Katie; 'of course not, but they *last* much longer.'

'Where was she bought?' asked Angela.

'In the Lowther Arcade,' said Katie.

'Ugh!' thought I; 'What a place to have come out of!' Mignonette sank lower and lower in my estimation.

'Where was *yours* bought, Angela?'

'Oh, at Cremer's in Regent Street,' said Angela. 'She was in the middle of the window, under a glass case, and she cost three guineas without her wardrobe.'

'Has she a wardrobe?' asked Katie, eyeing me again with awestruck admiration.

'Oh yes, of course. Hasn't Mignonette?'

'No; only the clothes she has on,' said Katie a little shyly – she saw how Angela looked down on her doll. 'But perhaps I

Improvised toys – the sound of the chair-race has even penetrated to the ground floor.

may get more by and by. I'm very fond of Mignonette, Angela, though, of course, she isn't like Victoria-Bess.'

'Oh, don't you think she's as pretty?' asked Angela in her cool way.

Dolls' houses imitative of every style of Victorian dwelling from terrace to palace were sold in ever-increasing numbers throughout the nineteenth century. One such as this would have been a little girl's pride and joy.

A little girl taking her doll out for a walk.

'Why, of course I don't,' said little Katie, speaking up with warmth and colouring slightly. 'I'm not so silly as to pretend I do; but Mignonette is made of much stronger stuff than *your* doll, Angela, and will very likely be nice and fresh-looking long after *she's* old and ugly.'

I felt indignant at the words 'age and ugliness' being mentioned in the same breath with my name, and would like to have smitten Katie for her impudence. Ah! I did not know then with what wisdom she spoke!

As the story progresses Victoria-Bess is supplanted in Angela's affections by a mechanical quacking duck that lays

The dolls' tea party – another perennial favourite occupation of young girls.

eggs, which her parents have brought from the Paris Exposition. Victoria-Bess has a fall, breaks her nose and is relegated to the top shelf of the toy cupboard. In time she is rescued from this obscurity, rejected as a 'nasty, dirty, broken-nosed, cracky old thing' by Angela and given to a children's hospital where she becomes the proud possession of a little girl called Moggy whose arm has been amputated:

> 'I have only *one* arm to nurse you with now, my queen – my beauty, but I'll love you ever so, and *lor*, how I'll prize you!'

As the pathos reaches boiling point, the little girl in the bed next to Moggy's leans across and whispers:

A game of cards – only in the most puritan of nineteenth-century
households were playing cards forbidden.

'Shall I show you *mine* now, Moggy? – she was brought to me when you was having your arm dressed, and the screen was round you.'

'Yes, I'd like to see 'er,' said Moggy.

The little girl held up a doll made of rag.

'She's very fresh and pink, ain't she?' said its mistress, 'considering she ain't a *new* doll?'

'Yes – a sweet pretty creature,' exclaimed Moggy. 'I'm sure she looks new every bit.'

'But she ain't,' said the little girl; 'the lady what brought me her, told me she had been played with over a year by a little girl what's dead now. And what do you think she told me the little girl had called her, Moggy? – You'd never guess – Mignonette!'

I turned my eyes with painful scrutiny towards the cot, and there recognized in the child's arms Katie's little rag doll, looking as fresh and blooming as the day I had first met her in Eaton Square, when she had come with Katie to drink tea with Angela and me. *Her* nose was not broken; *her* cheeks were not pale; *her* dress was not faded, and looking up at her with sad remorseful eyes, remembering how I had despised her in my days of insolent prosperity and pride, because she was made of *rag*, I remembered poor little Katie's words to Angela, and thought 'how true they have come!' –

'But Mignonette is made of much stronger stuff than *your* doll, Angela, and will very likely be nice and fresh-looking long after *she's* old and ugly!'

With one final appeal from Victoria-Bess to all little children to take their discarded toys to 'an Hospital for Sick Children' the book ends with a choking sob and a thundering moral.

Apart from dolls and soldiers, bricks, hoops and tops, the Victorian toy cupboard contained hobby-horses with and without wheels, tinplate models of trains and perambulators, and those by-products of the watchmaking industry – clockwork

The Victorian boy dressed as a coachman has coerced his little sisters to act as
horses – a game he apparently enjoys more than they do.

toys. There were dancing bears, tumbling clowns, roundabouts
and horses and carriages – a complete adult world in operational
miniature. Alongside these were the games – jigsaws, spillikins,
skittles, snakes and ladders, the Game of Goose, Happy Families,
checkers, draughts, the precursor of Monopoly – a finance game
called 'Moneta' – and the precursor of Scrabble – a word game
called 'Logos'. Card and board games lent themselves especially

to the didactic. Endless variations on the 'Happy Families' theme, for example, involved children in matching up plants, animals and birds in English, French and German, while war games often required a working knowledge of European history. One of the most famous of all toys – Noah's Ark – had been introduced originally in the sixteenth century, but achieved an enormous popularity in the nineteenth. In particularly religious households where the Sabbath was strictly observed, Noah's Ark was the only toy considered suitable for use on Sunday. For the rest of the week it rested on the top shelf of the toy cupboard whilst the other toys littered the nursery floor. It is hardly surprising that so many excellent examples have been preserved.

THE BOOKS.

'WHAT is the use of a book,' thought Alice,
'without pictures or conversations?'

Alice's Adventures in Wonderland, LEWIS CARROLL

THE nineteenth century saw an enormous boom in the writing and publication of children's books full of pictures and conversations, and the well-stocked nursery bookshelf certainly held more than just schoolbooks, medical encyclopaedias and the sort of book that Alice's sister was reading. The Victorians encouraged their children to read provided that they did not over-tire their eyes or neglect the exercise so necessary to their physical well-being. The other great proviso was, of course, that the books their children read should be 'good'.

Children are notoriously hard on books. Books written for adults can survive down the centuries in pristine condition, but children's favourite books soon fall to pieces – dog-eared and well-thumbed. One class of children's books that has survived in enormous numbers is the type of 'improving' novel issued by such bodies as the Religious Tract Society. Most of these stories are harmless enough tales adopting what was known as a 'high' moral tone. Reading the reviews of some of them, one can understand why so many of these volumes have survived in such good condition:

> *Through a Needle's Eye* by Hesba Stretton . . . tells in a pleasant manner the development of a man's character by misfortune and religious emotions. It has an interesting plot of clerical life in an English village, and one's attention is held throughout. There is a thoroughly wholesome tone about it and we are sure that it will be popular.

A story before bed – the tremendous boom in children's literature in the nineteenth century gave children, for the first time, a wide variety of books written especially for them.

Scenes in the Life of an Old Armchair – by Mrs Walton – The author has established a reputation for bright and pure writing, which may safely go in the hands of young folks. The vicissitudes of an old armchair have given scope for her fancy, and the story of its many occupants is full of interest . . . There is power in every chapter of the book, and the Christian teaching which it inculcates adds to the value it possesses as a literary work.

Sunday School Romances by Alfred B. Cooper – A series of stories of romantic incidents in the lives of persons connected with a certain Sunday School.

But reviews were written for parents and not for children. Many a Victorian child must have been sat down on a Sunday with one of these 'improving' tales to read. *Christie's Old Organ* by Mrs O. F. Walton is typical. The central character is an orphan boy, Christie, who befriends an old organ grinder called Treffy who has not long to live:

Old Treffy loved his barrel-organ; it was the one comfort of his life. He was a poor forlorn old man, without a friend in the world. Every one that he had ever loved was dead; and he had no one to whom he could talk, or to whom he could tell his troubles. And thus he gathered up all the remaining bits and fragments of love in his old heart, faded and withered though they were, and he gave them all to his old organ, which had well-nigh seen as many summers as he had. It was getting very antiquated and old-fashioned now; the red silk in front of it was very soiled and worn, and it could not play any of the new tunes of which the children were so fond. It sometimes struck old Treffy that he and his organ were very much alike – they were getting altogether behind the age; and people looked down on them and pushed past them, as they hurried along the street. And though old Treffy was very patient, yet he could not help feeling this.

Youth and age – children were encouraged in 'improving' stories to be
charitable to those less fortunate than themselves.

A sentimental portrayal of Victorian motherhood.

A reconstruction of a late Victorian nursery at Wallington House, Northumberland.

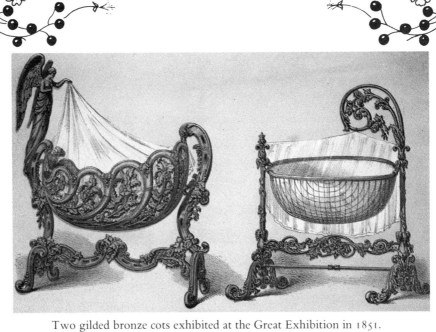

Two gilded bronze cots exhibited at the Great Exhibition in 1851.

These early nineteenth-century children are being taught to read by the village schoolmistress. She is using a horn book – presumably backed up with the other aids to learning so lovingly illustrated here!

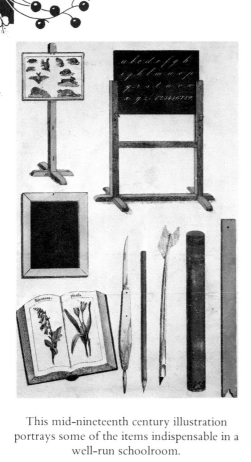

Bowling a wooden or metal hoop with a stick was one of the favourite games of Victorian children. One writer recalls the popularity of the pavement around the base of the Albert Memorial in London as a venue for hoop racing.

This mid-nineteenth century illustration portrays some of the items indispensable in a well-run schoolroom.

Sampler worked in coloured wools and silks by Jane
Elizabeth Morrison in 1863.

Brother and sister – painted in 1896 by the artist, Wardleworth. The
boy is dressed in a sailor suit and his sister wears a coral necklace – as
did so many little Victorian girls.

'Earth Stars' and 'But he was only sunk in a dream of light' – illustrations from *The Story without End*, a charming tale for children published in 1868. The illustrations are by E. V. R. Boyle.

Two illustrated songs from *The Baby's Opera* by Walter Crane. Between
1877 and 1887 Crane illustrated and decorated several books which enjoyed
an enormous popular success. This one contained fifty-six pages and sold at
five shillings.

The fifth musketeer – this little boy from the mid-nineteenth century would have worn a dress until he was at least four years old. The practice lasted well into the first decade of the present century.

Three performing clowns. This elaborate toy was a complete circus act in miniature, consisting of three articulated wooden clowns, two ladders, a barrel and a chair. The combinations were endless. (Photograph courtesy of Jeremy Cooper)

A group of Victorian toys – ranging from three rabbit skittles to a clockwork somersaulting mouse. (Photograph courtesy of Jeremy Cooper)

THE CAMEL.

Camel, patient, kind, and mild, teach me, though a little Child,
That obedient I must be,—patient, willing, just like thee;
Content with what falls to my share,—
And willing others' loads to bear.

A page from a Victorian child's picture book.

THE BOOKS.

To amuse or horrify? – The publication in 1823 of the translation of fairy stories by the brothers Grimm opened the floodgates to a torrent of fairy tales from every land. This illustration, entitled 'Fairy Ointment', comes from a collection of English stories published in 1890.

He had felt it very much on the day of which I am writing. It was cold, dismal weather; a cutting east wind had swept round the corners of the streets, and had chilled the old man through and through. His threadbare coat could not keep it out; how could he expect it to do so, when he had worn it so many years he could scarcely count them? His thin, trembling old hands were so benumbed with cold that he could scarcely feel the handle of the organ, and, as he turned it, he made sundry little shakes and quavers in the tune, which were certainly not intended by the maker of the old barrel-organ.

There was not much variety in the tunes old Treffy could play. There was the 'Old Hundredth', and 'Poor Mary Ann', and 'Rule Britannia'; the only other one was 'Home, Sweet Home', but that was Treffy's favourite. He always played it very slowly, to make it last longer, and on this cold day the shakes and quavers in it sounded most pathetic.

But no one took much notice of old Treffy or his organ. A little crowd of children gathered round him and asked him for all sorts of new tunes of which he had never even heard the names . . .

Poor old Treffy was almost fainting, but he must not give up, for he had not a halfpenny in his pocket, and he had come out without his breakfast. At length a kind-hearted farmer's wife, who was passing with a basket on her arm, took pity on the trembling old man, and gave him a penny from her capacious pocket . . .

At last as daylight was fading, he turned homeward. On his way he parted with his solitary penny for a cake of bread, and slowly and wearily he dragged himself up the steep stairs to his lonely attic . . .

He felt very cast down and dismal as he raked together the cinders, and tried to make a little blaze in the small fire he had lighted.

But when he had eaten his cake and taken some tea which he had warmed over again, old Treffy felt rather better, and he turned as usual to his old organ to cheer his fainting spirits. For old Treffy knew nothing of a better Comforter.

Unknown to old Treffy, the orphan boy, Christie, is sleeping on the doorstep of the house. He loves the sound of the organ and eventually meets its owner. Christie teaches the old man about the love of God and watches over him in his last, fatal illness – taking the barrel-organ onto the streets himself in order to earn money to feed them both. Left on his own, after Treffy's death, Christie, too, nearly dies of cold and hunger. However, he is just able to support himself by playing the organ until he is himself 'saved' by a city missionary who takes him in. In the fullness of time Christie becomes a helper in a country parish and marries.

'The Hunting of the Snark' – this illustration from Lewis Carroll's famous poem (1876) was executed by Henry Holiday. It is typical of the slightly macabre pictures which apparently delighted the Victorians.

OUR LITTLE FOLKS' OWN PUZZLES.

WORD PUZZLE.

WHAT is the meaning of the following?
ALLO

DOROTHY BEETON.
180, *Haverstock Hill, N.W.*　　(Aged 13.)

METAGRAM.

MY first is to cut down.
Change my head and I am to promise.
Again, and I am a line.
Again, and I am not high.
Again, and I am to drag.
Again, and I am to bend.
Again, and I am the present time.
Again, and I am an animal.

ERNEST F. POWELL.
(Aged 10.)
High Street, Shaftesbury.

CHARADES.

MY first is a farm produce.
My second is an insect.
My whole changes its being several times.

My first is an article of use.
My second is a piece of timber.
My whole may be found in the kitchen.

BORIS BERTHENSON.
(Aged 12.)
Sergeivskaia, 40, St. Petersburg.

PICTORIAL PUZZLE.

The central letters of the names of the objects represented above—placed in their proper order—will form the name of a vegetable.

DOUBLE GEOGRAPHICAL ACROSTIC.

MY initials, read downwards, form the name of a cathedral city of England; my finals, read upwards, form the name of a famous historical town in France.

1. A range of European mountains
2. A large island off China.
3. A famous volcano.
4. A river in France.
5. A province of Austria.
6. A country of South America.
7. A town in Brazil.

MARY A. WILLIAMS.
Dover College, Dover.　　(Aged 15.)

ALPHABET PUZZLE.

THE five asterisks of the left slant represent a well-known tree; the next slant, a stand for pictures; the next, something used for catching wild horses; the next, a vegetable. The larger asterisks will then give the name of a well-known fruit.

IRENE WEAR.
(Aged 14.)
6, *Stratford Grove, Newcastle-on-Tyne.*

BURIED NAMES OF ANIMALS.

1. DO eat, Gerald; you will feel better then.
2. For Blindman's Buff a lot of children are required.
3. Clara and I will play against Agnes and Bertie.
4. Is your brother at school already?
5. I put the cup on your table.
6. Oh, Leo! pardon me, I pray you.

ELSIE M. DAY.
(Aged 12.)
Glendwr, 52, Brixton Hill, London, S.W.

HIDDEN PROVERBS.

AAAACCCDDEEEEEEEEEEFF
HHHIKKLLLMNNNOOOPPRRS
SSTTTTTUVW.

AABCDEEEEFFFGHHIKLOOORRR
STTT.

GERALDINE E. BROAD.
(Aged 12½.)
Sunnyside, St. Germain's Road, Forest Hill, S.E.

MISSING LETTER PUZZLE.

WHEN the missing letters are supplied, the whole will form a verse from a poem by Longfellow.

"T×e×a×i×d×n×,a×d×h×d×r×n×s×
F×l×s×r×m×h×w×n×s×f×i×h×,
A×a×e×t×e×i×w×f×e×d×w×w×r×
F×o×a×e×g×e×n×i×f×i×h×."

IDA C. VARLEY.
(Aged 12.)
94, *Wharton Road, West Kensington Park, W.*

A puzzle page from a nineteenth-century children's magazine, *Little Folks* (1891).

THE BOOKS.

In the last sentences in the book he writes to his benefactor:

> And now, dear Mr Wilton, you may think of Nellie and me
> living together in love and happiness in the dear little earthly
> home, yet still looking forward to the eternal home above, our
> true, our best, our brightest 'Home, sweet Home!'

It is hardly surprising that the Victorian boy who had been
reading *Treasure Island* or *The Last of the Mohicans* from Monday
to Saturday should have given *Christie's Old Organ* scant atten-
tion on Sunday.

In 1823 there appeared the first collection of fairy stories to be
published in England. These were translations of those by the
brothers Grimm. Hans Christian Andersen's tales were translated and published in 1846 and the well-known collection of
fairy stories from all lands in several books of different colours
was edited by Andrew Lang and published at the turn of the
century. All these remained firm favourites well into the present
century. Classic children's books which are still widely read and
which first appeared in the nineteenth century include Edward
Lear's *Book of Nonsense* (1846), Carroll's *Alice's Adventures in
Wonderland* (1865) and *Through the Looking-glass* (1872),
Marryat's *Children of the New Forest* (1847), Cooper's *The Last of
the Mohicans* (1826), Ballantyne's *Coral Island* (1858) and Stevenson's *Treasure Island* (1883). In addition there were foreign
imports: *Little Women* by Louisa M. Alcott (1868), *The Swiss
Family Robinson* by J.R. Wyss (1814), *Heidi* by Johanna Spyri
(1881) and *Pinocchio* by Carlo Collodi (1882). Other classics
included many 'school' stories of which the most famous were
Tom Brown's School Days by Thomas Hughes (1857), *Eric; or
Little by Little* by Dean Farrar (1858), and *Vice Versa; A Lesson to
Fathers* by F. Anstey (1882). If we add to these the moral tales like
Pilgrim's Progress, Gulliver's Travels, The Fairchild Family by

Mary Martha Sherwood (1818) and Kingsley's *Water Babies* (1863), we can begin to get a picture of just how rich the Victorian children's library was.

The nineteenth century also saw the birth of the weekly and monthly journal. Many of these were aimed at Sunday readers and were consequently of 'high moral tone'. There were, for example, magazines like *Sundays at Home, Little Folks*, and *The Family Friend*, whose adventure stories were often only vehicles for some very unsubtle religious teaching. However, there were also magazines of a less 'wholesome' and more purely enjoyable nature. *Chatterbox* – a delightful confection of stories, quizzes and pictures – was first published in 1866 and *The Boy's Own Paper* and *The Girl's Own Paper* appeared in 1879 and 1880 respectively; and there were many others. Funny papers or comics also made their first appearance in the nineteenth century. *Fun* was first published in 1861, and *Thomas Hood's Comic Annual* in 1867. In addition there were *Ally Sloper's Half Holiday* and two comics – *Chips* and *Comic Cuts*, first issued in the nineties – which started the convention of strip cartoons with dialogue in bubbles. Regardless of whether the latter were encouraged in the average Victorian nursery, the children's bookshelf in the nineteenth century obviously did not need to be dull.

Improvements in colour printing techniques also resulted in the production of any number of beautifully illustrated children's books. Walter Crane's alphabet books started to appear from 1864 and books of nursery rhymes included *The Baby's Opera, The Baby's Bouquet* and *Pan Pipes* – all of which are masterpieces of their type. Victorian children, too, were regaled with 'pop-up' books and books with movable pictures, panoramic books and, at the turn of the century, rag books. All these were illustrated by highly competent artists and have now become collectors' items. Certainly the Victorian child was better off for books than his

CAUGHT!

Such a famous heap we
made,
Lil and I, with pail and spade;
Then we set, to guard the hill,
Her two dollies—Jack and Jill.

But, while we admired the
heap,
Up that sly old tide did creep;
Floated quickly o'er the sand,
Cut us all off from the land.

"Never mind me," cried poor
Lil;
"Save, oh, save my Jack and
Jill!"
But, 'mid many a squeal and
squall,
Ere they drowned, I saved
them all!

'Caught!' – an illustrated poem from *Little Folks* (1891).

predecessors and, arguably, than his descendants. However, there is unquestionably something sneaky about the didactic moralistic approach that infiltrated even the most innocent-looking children's literature:

ABOUT OYSTERS

To forgive injuries is a great thing, but to turn them into blessings is a greater. Now there is one little animal that turns a wound into a pearl, and this little animal – the oyster – is really without a head, and hence called *acephalous*; but I think we shall admit that it puts to shame many an animal that *has a head*.

Then this little animal, instead of manifesting any resentment when it is crudely scooped from its shell, lies at rest in the human stomach, and mixes most readily with its juices, so as to be easily absorbed into the human system. Being thus so perfectly digestible, the oyster is of great use to invalids, and those who can take no other kind of food. The oyster is very widely diffused, being found in most of the seas of Europe, and other parts of the world. In some seas it forms immense banks, which protect exposed coasts from strong currents. One oyster bed in the English Channel is above forty miles long, and is worked during the season by more than a hundred boats which convey their cargoes to all parts of Europe. These deep-sea oysters, however, are rather large and coarse compared with the delicious little plump ones, called 'natives'. The largest and coarsest oysters are called 'roughs'; those of middling size are known as 'commons'; and the 'natives' are the small ones that are found only in the mouths of some of the rivers of Kent and Essex . . .

The spawn of the oyster comprises a number of bright little eggs, that float about in little greenish lumps. In time these lumps burst, and each little egg is then furnished with a small

MY
LIT-
·TLE
BRO-
·THER

WHOM
I
LOVE

SITS
BE-
LOW

AND
I
SING
A=
=BOVE

'The Rose Tree' – a delightful illustration from a children's book at the turn of the century, showing the influence of the fashionable Romantic school of painting.

fringe of hair. By help of this it floats and grows, becoming more and more of the shape of an oyster, until the little hairs become hardened into layers of shell, and the young oyster then settles down to a steady and quiet life on some rock, or in some nice bed of mud. Here it lies and grows for three years when it becomes large enough to be taken as food for man.

The oyster has many enemies during its youthful days. Mr

BLOW·WIND·BLOW·

Blow, wind, blow! and go, mill, go!
  That the miller may grind his corn;
That the baker may take it, and into rolls make it,
  And send us some hot in the morn.

Beautifully illustrated books of nursery rhymes proliferated towards the end of the nineteenth century. These two pages come from *The Big Book of Nursery Rhymes*, which was illustrated by Charles Robinson (*c.*1890).

WINTER·HAS·COME

Cold and raw
the north
wind doth blow,

Bleak in a morning
early;

All the hills are covered
with snow,

And winter's now come
fairly.

(107)

Fivefingers (the starfish) is very fond of poking one of its limbs, or fingers, between the shells, when it finds a chance. But the oyster is sometimes quick enough to shut its valves off with such force as to snap off the intruder's limb, and Mr Fivefingers thus becomes Mr Fourfingers. Mr Crab is also a great enemy to the poor oyster – poking its claws, or sharp feet into the soft body of the oyster, whenever it sees the shells open. These hard limbs are not so easily snapped, and the poor oyster, becoming exhausted, relaxes its pressure, whereupon the bulgarious crab pokes and scoops away as effectively as any one of Sweeting's useful openers! . . .

Our consumption of oysters is mostly the eating of them from the shell, as we term it, and as a sauce to cod-fish . . .

The oyster that produces the pearl is found in the Indian seas at Ceylon, where the pearl fishery has long been carried on, but is so precarious as to be unattractive to the steady industry of Europeans. Hundreds and hundreds of oysters are taken without yielding any but a few small, or *seed-pearls*. A pearl the size of a pea is worth some few pounds, according to its colour and shape. The few large pearls, of the size of a pigeon's egg, that have been found, are as well-known as the Koh-i-noor and other famous diamonds. The celebrated Hope-pearl is the largest, and is valued at an immense sum on account of its rarity. The procuring of 'a pearl of great price', as a provision against want, will occur to the mind of every Bible reader.

ANSWERS TO OUR LITTLE FOLKS' OWN PUZZLES (*p.* 100).

WORD PUZZLE.
Nothing after all.

METAGRAM.
Mow. Vow. Row. Low. Tow. Bow. Now. Cow.

CHARADES.
BUTTERFLY—CUPBOARD.

DOUBLE GEOGRAPHICAL ACROSTIC.
CHESTER—ORLEANS.
1. C aucasu S. 2. H aina N.

3. E tn A. 4. S ein E. 5. T yro L.
6. E cuado R. 7. R io de Janeir O.

ALPHABET PUZZLE.
MELON.

```
  M       L       N
    A   E A   O
    P   S   S   I
      L A     S N
        E     O
```

BURIED NAMES OF ANIMALS.
1. Doe. 2. Buffalo. 3. Stag. 4. Rat. 5. Pony. 6. Leopard.

HIDDEN PROVERBS.
" Take care of the pence, and the pounds will take care of themselves."
"Birds of a feather flock together."

MISSING LETTER PUZZLE.
" The day is done, and the darkness
Falls from the wings of Night,
As a feather is wafted downward
From an eagle in his flight."

PICTORIAL PUZZLE.
POTATO.
Foun T ains. St O rk. Sta T ion.
C O w. A P e. Pyr A mid.

THE BOOKS.

The largest oyster pearl is what all the world would buy; the heavenly 'pearl of great price' is what all the world cannot give, and yet it may be obtained by even the very poorest, who by it becomes 'rich in faith' and 'an inheritor of the Kingdom of Heaven'.

The Family Friend, August 1871

Not all Victorian children's books were quite so didactic and the Victorians themselves realized as well as anyone just how much children enjoyed stories about children. In *The Magic Half Crown* there is a nursery scene that must have delighted children one hundred years ago by its very familiarity:

Early in the afternoon of the following day, snow began to fall in large feathery flakes, and very soon the roofs of buildings, the stems of trees, and the tops of walls were covered with soft white cushions. Snow piled itself up in corners outside the windows of Elsie Marshall's nursery, and her cat, Bridget, having taken a walk to look for an unwary bird, found the return journey through the snow very unpleasant and somewhat fatiguing . . .

The nursery fire was bright and cheerful, and a kettle was singing on the hob in preparation for the nursery tea. Nurse, sitting by the window, with a view to getting the best light she could, was busily mending stockings. Elsie Marshall and Margaret Neville, her little Indian cousin, were arranging a collection of dolls of various sizes, makes and degrees of beauty. At least Elsie was arranging the dolls, and Margaret was acting the part of useful and willing help, when she was not beguiled by her interest in watching the falling snow . . .

'How pretty the snow is!' cried Margaret; 'it looks like feathers constantly coming down from the skies.'

'Don't you know,' said Nurse, 'they are plucking geese in Yorkshire, and sending the feathers here!'

'Are they?' said Margaret, astonished, and opening her large eyes wide.

'Nurse is only making fun of you, Margaret,' said Elsie; 'she used to make me believe that rubbish.'

How perfect the scene is and how beautifully made for children. Elsie's Indian cousin has never seen snow before and so every young English reader feels slightly superior to her; and how many Victorian families had pet cats, dolls, nursery teas and nannies' little jokes!

Certainly Victorian children were not short of bedtime stories or any other time stories for that matter.

THE CLOTHES.

JOY to Philip, he this day
Has his long coats cast away,
And (the childish season gone)
Puts the manly breeches on.

'Going into Breeches,' CHARLES AND MARY LAMB

ARGUMENTS about how children should be dressed raged throughout the nineteenth century. On one side there were the advocates of practical clothing which allowed children to behave like children – a far larger and more vociferous band than is often supposed – and on the other, the slavish followers of fashion for whom the tenet 'il faut souffrir pour être belle' was one of the accepted facts of life. On the whole the latter faction had their way in the dressing of little girls and the former in choosing boy's clothes. A Victorian children's wardrobe of the 1860s might well have contained a crinoline and pantaloons for a little girl, but a practical, comfortable sailor suit for her brother.

Nevertheless, for the first six or so years of their lives, both boys and girls would have looked almost identical in their little skirts with or without pantaloons, and it must indeed have been a joyous day for a Victorian boy when he cast off skirts in favour of the more manly breeches.

Controversy about clothing, though, did not start when the child reached the age of being 'breeched'. There were many schools of thought on the subject of baby clothing. In *An Encyclopaedia of Domestic Economy* by Thomas Webster and Mrs Parkes, which appeared in 1844, the authors inveighed against the common practice of swaddling babies:

The use of all bandages, swaddling clothes, tight ligatures, is most carefully to be forbidden . . . the clothing of infants should be warm, light and loose . . . that kind should be employed which may seem best adapted to secure the equal and tranquil diffusion of the blood throughout the system.

The length of babies' clothes also upset them:

Infants for the first three or four months are clothed in very long petticoats . . . they help to keep the feet of the infant safe from cold air, which would otherwise chill an infant very severely, and long clothes do also give a nurse a good hold of a child, who without sufficient clothing would be apt to slip out

Highland costumes for children were popularized in the 1850s by the Royal Family, who bought Balmoral in 1851 and started to dress their children in tartan.

Two sporting costumes for boys advertised by Messrs Peter Robinson in 1892.

36. Reefer Coat, to fit over skirts ... ... from **8 6**
53. Undress Scotch Suit, in a variety of fancy Tweeds and Serge ... ,, **12/6**
57. The "Newmarket," for Boys of three to eight years... ... ... ,, **27/6**

48. The "Golf" Suit, in Fancy Tweed, with Box-cloth Continuations ... from **25 -**
7. Eton Suit, with Black or Grey Trousers ... ... ,, **35 -**
11. School Suit, in Fancy Tweed or Black Worsted ... ... ,, **19 6**

Coats and suits – boys' clothes suitable for winter wear (1892).

NOVELTIES IN CHILDREN'S COSTUMES.

Hats and frocks – girl's clothes suitable for summer wear (1892).

of her arms, but to have them so long as to trail on the ground, or to float with every move made by the nurse, so as to reach the bars of the grate, is preposterous, and even dangerous, and the good sense of every mother ought to be exerted to lay aside this worthless fashion.

Mrs J.E. Panton, in her *Hints for Young Householders or From Kitchen to Garret*, gives a list for a layette of the 1880s:

> 12 very fine lawn shirts, 10 long flannels, 6 fine long cloth petticoats, 8 monthly gowns, 8 nightgowns, 4 head flannels, a large flannel shawl, 6 dozen large Russian diapers, 6 good flannel pilches, 3 or 4 pairs tiny woollen shoes.

Fashions in almost every sphere of Victorian activity were often dictated by what the Queen herself and the Royal Family did, and the fashionable way of dressing children was no exception. When the Royal Family bought Balmoral in 1851 there ensued what one writer has called 'Balmoralomania' in the field of children's costume. At the opening of the Great Exhibition the young Prince Edward appeared with his parents in full Highland dress and at the wedding of the Princess Royal in 1858, four young princes sported tartan outfits. The Victorian public were not slow to follow the new fashion. Tartan became instantly desirable for dressing both boys and girls – whether it was a full Highland costume, a dress or even a simple sash.

The Royal Family, too, were responsible for the one children's fashion that typifies the Victorian era above all other – the sailor suit. In 1846 the court painter Winterhalter portrayed the Prince of Wales in a complete replica of an adult sailor's suit. The young Prince had appeared wearing it on the deck of the royal yacht, *Victoria and Albert*, that year during a royal visit to Ireland, to the intense delight of the crowds, and the costume became an instant success. The Prince's original sailor suit had been made by a Bond Street tailor and was a faithful replica of the genuine article

High fashion – some girls' dresses at the end of the nineteenth century were beginning to show a tendency towards a style that allowed more freedom of movement.

– complete with bell-bottom trousers, lanyards and black boater. Later imitations of it, however, became far less accurate until the outfit was eventually worn by girls and boys alike, the former having sailor skirts below the tunic top. As a fashion, though, it spread throughout Europe and lasted perhaps longer than any other – well into the present century. By the 1880s, sailor suits were almost a uniform for boys. They were ideal wear, being

NOVELTIES
IN
Children's
MANTLES.

ALICE.—Child's Cape in various colours.

NORA.—In Fancy Tweeds First size, **45 6.**

NANCY.—In Plain Cloths. First Size, **15 9.**

MILDRED.—In Plain and Fancy Cloths, **28 6.**

SYBIL.—In Plain Colours. First Size, **25 6.**

ETHEL.—In Fancy Cloths First Size, **42 -.**

Cloaks for little girls were popular throughout the Victorian period, and illustrations from *Little Red Riding Hood* frequently served as models for their design.

Fancy-dress balls became extremely fashionable towards the end of the nineteenth century and this illustration from a society magazine of the period shows just how much variety was available in children's costumes.

comfortable, tidy and – best of all – jingoistic. What Victorian father walking his family in Hyde Park and seeing his own and other children sporting their blue-and-white naval uniforms could forget that Britannia ruled the waves!

In an article in *Woman's World* for 1888, Mrs Oscar Wilde put her finger on the reason for another fashion in children's clothes having such a wide currency:

> It is probably owing to artists having turned their attentions to matters of dress that we see so many picturesquely dressed children around us. Many of these dresses are historical, and the favourite dress for both boys and girls seems to be the Charles I dress. We have little Cavaliers in plush tunics and knickerbockers with coloured silk sashes and Vandyck collars.

Historical dress was indeed all the rage for children in the 1880s, but Mrs Wilde might have narrowed the instigators down to just one – Reginald Birch, the illustrator of Frances Hodgson Burnett's immensely successful novel – *Little Lord Fauntleroy*. This first appeared in serial form in America in 1885, was published in England as a book in 1886 and had an instantaneous success. It was translated into more than a dozen languages, selling over a million copies in England alone and earning for its author something well in excess of $100,000. Birch took his cue from one classic description of Cedric's outfit:

> What the Earl saw was a graceful childish figure in a black velvet suit with a lace collar, and with lovelocks waving about his handsome, manly little face.

In fact the grand 'Fauntleroy' suit was originally run up for Cedric by the maid, Mary, out of an old velvet dress belonging to his mother, 'Dearest'. But this did not deter Victorian mothers, who copied the illustrator rather than the author in producing

The fashion for the sailor suit was started by the Royal Family when the Prince of Wales appeared in public wearing one in 1846.

Little Lord Fauntleroy – this portrait of the famous fictional hero lovingly depicts the costume which became a model for boys' party clothes in the 1880s.

more and more magnificent Cavalier outfits for their sons. Neither did they restrict themselves to the sombre black of the original. An advertisement in *The Lady* announced a capital outfit for 'a little fellow of seven . . . tunic and knickerbockers of sapphire blue velvet and sash of pale pink . . . Vandyck collar and cuffs of old point lace'. Such a costume, worn mainly for parties, might well have been finished off with a large feathered Cavalier hat – again taken from Birch's illustration. It is hardly surprising to find many young Victorians rebelling against such a ludicrous outfit. One of the first to do so was the authoress's own son, Vivian, and one of the last was Compton Mackenzie:

> That confounded Little Lord Fauntleroy craze which led to my being given as a party dress the Little Lord Fauntleroy costume of black velvet and Vandyck collar . . . Naturally the other boys were inclined to giggle at my black velvet, and after protesting in vain against being made to wear it I decided to make it unwearable by flinging myself down in the gutter on the way to the dancing-class and cutting the breeches, and incidentally severely grazing my own knees. I also managed to tear the Vandyck collar. Thus not only did I avoid the dancing-class, but I also avoided being photographed in that infernal get-up.

Little Victorian girls fared better in the matter of literature-inspired fashions. Over their simple frocks and pinafores inspired by Tenniel's illustrations for the Alice books, they might well have worn a warm and comfortable hooded cape inspired by the classic tale of 'Little Red Riding Hood'. Both were extremely popular in the nineteenth century and had the advantage, unlike the Fauntleroy suit, of being practical and unrestricting. They were also sharply contrasted with the heavy, dark dresses that so many little girls had to wear for much of the time.

Another Victorian illustrator who was responsible for starting a fashion in children's clothing – particularly girls' clothing – was Kate Greenaway. Her aesthetic drawings had an enormous effect on children's dress, and with the support of Arthur Lasenby

Mother and daughters, father and sons – one Victorian cartoonist saw more than a passing similarity between the clothes of children and those of their parents.

Some Victorian outfits even managed to combine several fashions at once. While the little girl wears a full tartan sash, her brother sports a costume that blends the black velvet Fauntleroy suit with the white stripes and ribbons of the sailor suit. Just for good measure he has buckle shoes and a bow tie.

This advertisement from the 1880s shows that children as well as adults might be expected to wear corsets.

Little Kate Greenaways – the aesthetic look for children's clothes in the 1880s ran concurrently with more sober fashions.

Liberty and his shop in Regent Street the 'Greenaway' look for Victorian girls became all the rage.

In the 1880s great advances were made in fabric manufacture. Dr Gustav Jaeger's Sanitary Woollen System popularized the idea of light woollen clothing worn next to the skin for warmth and health. Among early devotees of the idea were Oscar Wilde and George Bernard Shaw. Simultaneously with Dr Jaeger's innovations two English cotton-based materials – Aertex and Viyella – came into production in 1888 and 1891 respectively. At the same time, a predeliction for white and light colours also became fashionable.

By the turn of the century many of the less comfortable and more sombre fashions for children had been abandoned in favour of clothing more suited to a child's way of life. Boys began to wear shorts with their sailor-suit tops and girls' dresses were simple, unrestricting affairs in sharp contrast to the tightly-corseted extravagances they would have to wear as adults.

Two pages from a mid-nineteenth century spelling book.

A page from a Victorian child's
picture book.

This is the Palace the Prince built.

And this is the Man submitting his plan
To the Prince who approved, and said it was good,
That a Palace of Glass should be built on the grass,
For the great World's Fair, which has since been held there
And that Palace so famed, is everywhere named,
The fine Crystal Palace the Prince built.

A parody of a nursery rhyme marks the
building of the Crystal Palace (1851).

A MAN-OF-WAR.

"The wooden Walls of England," is a name
given to our ships of war. They differ in size,
some are very large and some small. A first-
rate line of battle ship, which is shown in the
picture, is very large; and carries eight or nine
hundred sailors and officers, with food enough
to supply them for several months; as well as
water, coals, gunpowder, and other stores.

Some very large ships carry one hundred
and twenty guns.

"I'SE GOOD"

MEETING OF THE TOTAL ABSTINENCE SOCIETY

"I COULDN'T, DOGGIE"

"TELL US A STORY WITH A CAKE IN IT"

"I'SE DOT A PARTNER"

"WE'RE ENGAGED"

"ME LOVES 'OO"

THE OLD LOVE AND THE NEW

Victorian parents were divided into two schools – the 'children should be seen and not heard' type, and the hopelessly sentimental. This early nineteenth-century series of drawings gives a glimpse of the latter. Adherents of the former school would have found the baby talk captions about as unpalatable as the idea of children sitting on the sideboard!

MARE AND FOAL.

Madam Mare, how do you do? proud of your foal no doubt are you.
He looks well formed, is sleek and slim, his tail is long, his mane is
trim.
    Bring him up well, and teach him his duty,
    Nor let him grow vain of his grace and his beauty.

Few young animals look more interesting than the foal, which, while young, is particularly
lively and playful; so much so as to give rise to the saying, "as lively as a colt." The Mare
is a kind and watchful mother, and is very attentive to her offspring. When taken from the
Mare to be broken in, as it is called, the Foal is trained to the particular kind of use or work
for which it is most adapted, and then for the first time, is made to know the use of the bit,
by which its driver is enabled to control its course, and direct its movements.

A page from a Victorian
picture book.

Illustrations from *Flora's Feast,* one of Walter Crane's later books, published in
1889. The idea of a pageant of flowers undoubtedly inspired
Cicely Mary Barker to compile her later *Flower Fairies.*

The dancing cat. Automata – very popular in the eighteenth century –
became cheaper and more readily available in the nineteenth. This toy
was made in Germany at the end of the Victorian period. (Photograph
courtesy of Jeremy Cooper)

The jockey wrestlers – this charming toy of the marionette type was
made in 1880. (Photograph courtesy of Jeremy Cooper)

(Above left) Weighing the kitten -- an illustration from *Chatterbox,* a
children's magazine from the late nineteenth century.
'Jack Spratt': (above right) a page from a collection of nursery rhymes
published in 1900 and illustrated by Chester Loomis. (Below) the same
rhyme, taken from *Ridicula Rediviva,* a curious collection published in 1869;
the Victorians' passionate interest in the Gothic is plainly seen.

This race game, of
French origin, begins
when the lever in
front of the case is
pulled; the pot in the
middle is for wagers.
The game was not
universally approved
of. (Photograph
courtesy of Jeremy
Cooper)

A visit to the
cobbler's shop – this
rather emancipated
nurse-maid has
brought her charge
to collect the other
shoe from the
cobbler.

A collection of late Victorian toys—
including a top, board games, and a popular
money box. (Photograph courtesy of
Jeremy Cooper)

Children were educated from earliest
youth to be charitable – whether through a
cup of tea to an old man or a florin to a
flower-girl.

THE
PHOTOGRAPH ALBUM.

To judge by the huge numbers of Victorian portrait photographs still extant, visits to the photographer's must have been frequent occurrences in the life of the middle-class family. How so many children managed to look vaguely at ease in these photographs is a miracle for it cannot have been a happy experience for them. Squeezed into their best party dresses or suits, these little Victorians had to sit or stand bolt upright for the interminable length of time it took for the exposure to be correct. Sometimes their necks were supported from behind in a type of caliper brace which made movement of the head impossible and at others they had to hold relaxed poses for aching minutes.

The business of trying to keep a very young child still for any length of time was just as much a problem to Victorian parents as

Photographing the first-born.

it is today. However, they managed it somehow and the results give a tantalizing glimpse of the Victorian child as his proud relations saw him – the hope of the future in an often theatrical setting in the photographer's studio far removed from the nursery or schoolroom that was his natural habitat.

A. 610.

2.

THE SCHOOLROOM.

A CHILD should always say what's true
And speak when he is spoken to,
And behave mannerly at table:
At least as far as he is able.

'Whole Duty of Children', ROBERT LOUIS STEVENSON

WHEN the Victorian child reached the age of five or six the
question of serious education arose. Children of poorer families
would already be attending ragged schools, village schools or
'dame schools' as they were often called. These institutions only
received a minimal Government grant from 1833 and were
largely dependent upon charity. Classes could be large and the
village schoolmistress needed great strength of character as well
as the patience of a saint and the constitution of an ox – a
formidable combination and one which made her a force to be
reckoned with.

In every village marked with little spire,
Embowered in trees, and hardly known to fame,
There dwells, in lowly cot, and mean attire,
A matron old, whom we schoolmistress name;
Her cap, far whiter than the driven snow,
Emblem right meet of decency does yield;
Her apron neatly trimmed, as blue, I trow,
As is the harebell that adorns the field.

'The Village Schoolmistress', ANON.

The village schoolmaster was also a stock Victorian character
as a glance at any of Mulready's school pictures shows. He, too,

had to be patient and long-suffering. For a pittance of a salary he had one of the least enviable of all jobs.

Relying largely upon charity as they did, these village schools were pitifully short of equipment and books. The high price of paper necessitated the use of slates and chalk, and visual aids were at a premium. Nevertheless, the charity schools did the best they could within these confines to give their pupils the three R's of elementary education.

For children of the middle classes things were quite different. Throughout the century boys were sent in ever-increasing numbers to public school. But the shortage of good schools for girls led to most of them being educated at home under the supervision of a governess. She was probably no better paid than the village schoolmistress, and also had to teach both boys and

An early Victorian illustration showing a father instructing his children in religious knowledge.

THE SCHOOLROOM.

The Book of Experiments – this frontispiece from an early nineteenth-century school book insists that science can be fun.

(144)

girls until the former went away to school, but socially she was a cut above her fellow teachers and, provided that she got on well with the cook, she was probably better fed. In larger establishments, too, she might have had the company of a tutor.

There can be no doubt that the Victorians would have been well advised to spend more time and money on their children's education. That they did not is apparent in the countless diatribes against the current education system in books and pamphlets which appeared throughout the century. From Mr Squeers's establishment to the schoolrooms of the most impressive residences, the hallmarks of Victorian education were a shortage of teaching aids and an army of under-paid, under-qualified teaching staff. The Rev. Anthony Thomson, for example, in his book *The English Schoolroom*, gives us a depressing picture:

> The rooms usually set apart as schoolrooms in houses of any pretension, and even of great pretension, are, in most instances, the very worst that can be picked out. They are mostly the dullest, the dampest, the poorest, or the most useless chambers in the whole building. 'Any room is good enough for a schoolroom' – such is the almost universal cry when arranging the accommodation of a great house; and even when such is being built, schoolrooms are about the last chambers to be considered.

Having detailed the appearance and positioning of the average Victorian schoolroom, Mr Thomson goes on to describe what he considers to be the perfect arrangement – one that was not found in many nineteenth century houses:

> Presuming the mansion is built with a centre and wings much after the fashion of the letter H, we would endeavour to secure a portion of one of the wings, on the garden front, remote from the grand approach, the reception rooms and the offices . . .

The village school – two illustrations from a Victorian tale about a 'ragged' school. First the boys are taken into the school and then their father visits them there.

THE SCHOOLROOM.

THE SCHOOLROOM.

On entering the schoolroom it would be seen that it was a long lofty room, with a sort of daïs at each end, and in the centre such a kind of fire-place stove as is to be seen in the British Museum, the Library of the Inner Temple, etc. This kind of stove consists of two open fire-places set back to back, the flue from which descends through the floor. The object of choosing such a stove is to assist the ventilation of the room, and to allow the bright, open, cheerful fire to be seen. Nothing is so depressing as those hideous black stoves, which either get insufferably hot, or afford no heat whatever . . .

Facing these fire-places should be the table-desks of the tutor and the governess, and on either side of each table-desk should be placed two other tables – the whole being arranged so as to form a hollow square, the centre occupied by the fire-place . . .

The wall-space between the windows should be occupied by bookcases, closed by doors, the panels of which should be filled by strong brass trellis work, so that the titles, state, etc., of the books within may be clearly seen. Each bookcase should rest on two drawers, furnished with locks, for the reception of papers, pens, pencils, etc. Below should be a cupboard without shelves for slates, atlases, portfolios, etc.

On the wall-space opposite the windows should hang black boards, maps, etc. and there should also be large slates, set in frames, which permit of adjustment to any given height . . .

On the daïs opposite the tutor should stand a small organ of two rows of keys, and fully supplied with pedals . . . It should have a distinct swell, however small, and the bellows should be worked by the simple hydraulic apparatus now so commonly in use . . .

On the daïs opposite the governess should stand a good grand piano, a harp, or a small harmonium, according to the taste of the parent. Such would be the general appearance of the schoolroom.

How Victorian parents' eyes must have opened at the descrip-

'Green Gravel' – a popular song from the illustrated *Children's Singing Games* which was published in the late nineteenth century. The influence of Kate Greenaway can clearly be seen in the design of the children's costumes.

tion of such a schoolroom! For most middle-class families even a separate room for the older children would have been a luxury. Many had to do the best they could by converting the day nursery, if there were no younger children, and otherwise giving over a downstairs room for lessons.

They might, however, have been more able to appreciate Mr Thomson's description of an ideal schoolroom library. Many of the books and types of books he mentions were certainly in general circulation:

> The lower shelves of the school library should be stocked with illustrated books of all kinds, from the simplest picture book to works containing views of foreign countries, works on natural history, mechanical arts, etc. The younger children will never tire of looking over these books, and acquire by the very inspection of them an immense fund of useful knowledge. Of course they must, in a great degree, be superintended by their 'guardians', to prevent damage, and the abuse of their much-coveted privilege of *'turning over for themselves'.*
>
> The middle shelves should be filled with the many excellent works of boyish adventure now current, and with the simpler forms of fiction, such as is represented by Miss Edgeworth's works, and minor history . . . The higher shelves may be dedicated to healthy grown fiction – such as Sir Walter Scott's novels (especially) – and our great essayists. Then will come historians, selections from our poets, and the usual books of our old writers – such as Izaak Walton, Fuller, Herbert, but above all Shakespeare (Knight's edition). We shall do well to add several illustrated works – for example, 'The Pictorial History of England', and the many excellent and pleasant books that treat of our own country, not merely as it was, but as it is . . .
>
> A shelf, too, should be dedicated to works of popular science, chemistry, geology, and botany. For example, Spencer Thomson's 'Wanderings among the Wild Flowers',

'The Chemistry of Common Life', Maury's 'Physical Geography of the Sea', Hugh Miller's works on geology; and such books as Pepper's 'Playbook of Science', Piesse's book on the application of Chemistry to parlour magic, etc. should find a place on this shelf.

Last, not least, should come a division entirely devoted to matters bearing on religion, as well as direct religious books. It will be as well if this division be kept apart ranged side by side with the Bible and Prayer-Book, and like them for *every-day use* – not, in any wise, to be imprisoned all the week, and only to be brought out on Sunday.

As the writer intimates, however, the vast majority of Victorian children would never enjoy so well-appointed a schoolroom or so well-stocked a schoolroom library. Most parents in the nineteenth century were content to closet their children in an attic room with a governess and a handful of books and to hope for the best. A great deal depended on the governess and surprisingly a great number rose to the occasion, providing their charges at least with the ability to take their places either at public school, in the case of twelve-year-old boys, or in society, in the case of eighteen-year-old girls. They appear to have achieved this by diluting discipline with affection and academicism with a long draught of practical knowledge – and all this in a not very strenuous working day.

Family routines vary considerably, but a fairly typical day in the Victorian schoolroom started at nine o'clock with lessons until noon. These three hours were generally devoted to purely academic subjects. Lunch was eaten either in the nursery or, in some cases, in the servant's hall. Only on very rare occasions did the children eat in the dining room with their parents before they were 'of an age', although in many families there was a long-standing custom that the children joined their parents for dessert in the evening, dressed, of course, in their best.

The Astley Cooper chair – Sir Astley Paston Cooper (1768–1841), the eminent surgeon and anatomist, developed this chair to correct faulty posture in children. It was impossible for a child not to sit bolt upright on it. Although several equally eminent anatomists fulminated against the chair throughout the century, it continued to be used and examples can still be found today.

Any opportunity to get even a few mouthfuls downstairs must have been a welcome treat for Victorian children. While adult meals in the nineteenth century were noted for their lavishness, those taken in the nursery were unbelievably dull. Boiled mutton seems to have been one of the staple dishes and the method of cooking it sounds appalling:

> It is usual in boiling meat to immerse it in cold or lukewarm water, and raise it gradually to a little below boiling point, where it is maintained until the cooking is complete.

Sealing the meat by rapid cooking was looked down upon by Victorian cooks as it did not produce the broth that was also extensively served in the nursery. Twentieth-century children

A meal in the dining room – Victorian children normally had their meals with the nurse or governess in the nursery. Only on very rare occasions did they eat with their parents in the dining room downstairs.

can consider themselves lucky that they are not fed according to a nineteenth-century dietary:

7.30 am.	first meal	– A breakfast-cupful of new milk, a rusk or a good slice of stale bread.
11.00 am.	second meal	– A cup of milk.
1.00 pm.	third meal	– A small slice of underdone mutton, one well-mashed potato, with a little gravy without fat, milk, water or milk and water.
6.00 pm.	fourth meal	– A breakfast-cupful of milk and bread and butter.

One of the subjects that a young lady learned in the schoolroom was drawing from life. A younger sister made a perfect model.

Off to school – most Victorian girls were educated at home, but boys tended increasingly to be sent away to a public school when they reached the age of twelve or so.

As an alternative to the mutton, beef-tea was also suggested. On rare occasions, too, the child might be given 'a table-spoonful of plain custard or farinaceous pudding'.

After lunch and a rest there would have been a walk, weather permitting, and the governess was expected to take the opportunity of this time to instruct her charges in basic botany and biology as well as collecting flowers to press and bugs to study.

Instead of or after the walk, there might well have been a dancing or a piano lesson. The children were encouraged to prepare pieces for performance to their parents and friends and a good governess would also be expected to be a fair pianist. Indeed, music played a large part in the education of children of all ages. From the singing games of the nursery to the more formal piano lessons of the schoolroom, children were encouraged to appreciate the best in contemporary composition. The preface to a collection of *Songs for the Schoolroom*, published in 1869 states:

> The design of this work is to furnish chaste and elegant melodies, calculated to lay the foundation for a pure and correct taste in music.

By the time a child left the Victorian nursery, he or she would be ready to take a seat at any one of the many concerts that were such a feature of nineteenth-century life. In addition, piano-playing and singing at private musical soirées would hold no terrors. At the drop of the lightest hint the young Victorian would produce a copy of a popular humoresque or ballad and launch into it.

At the end of the afternoon there was still one more hour's work to be done between four and five o'clock. This concluded the formal part of the day's education, but Victorian children were encouraged to continue their studies more informally until bedtime. Naturally the governess was required to supervise.

THE GOVERNESS.

HOW delightful it would be to be a governess!
to go out into the world; to enter a new life;
to act for myself; to exercise my unusual faculties;
to earn my own maintenance.

Agnes Grey, ANNE BRONTË

ONCE a child had reached the age of eighteen or had started life at a public school, it must have seemed a long, long time ago that he or she first entered the schoolroom and first met the new governess. So many Victorian writers, however, recalled that moment in later life, that one is forced to realize just how traumatic it must have been. To leave the nursery for the schoolroom and nurse for a governess was a small death for a five-year-old child as Lady Sybil Lubbock remembers in her autobiography, *The Child in the Crystal:*

When we reached home after those Harewood holidays what did we find? Not the comfortable nursery under the easy rule of our Highland Nanny, but a properly ordered schoolroom beneath the quiet and careful supervision of our new English governess . . . Nanny had gone, had gone for good and to Australia, most remote of all continents. The bottom fell out of my small safe world – I had never imagined that such calamity could befall me. I knew of course that most girls of our age had governesses and not nurses; nor had I failed to observe that there was frequent friction between Nanny and my sister, Joan seeing herself too old for nursery discipline, Nanny unwilling to relinquish her authority. But children do not look far ahead – what has been will surely not cease to be; so that when I returned from an outing – it was, I think, a visit

with some cousins to the French Exhibition at Earl's Court –
and found Nanny gone, it was as if a thunderbolt had struck
my house of life and shattered it to fragments . . .

I have had my share of sorrow – who has not? – but nothing,

Not all Victorian establishments were large enough to have a separate schoolroom or a resident governess. This little boy is being taught by a visiting or
'daily' governess at a corner of the dining room table.

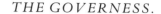

I truly think, has ever equalled the intensity of that first grief, the blackness of that first despair.

Lady Lubbock's reaction to leaving the nursery was by no means exceptional. Over and over again in the literature of the period the Victorian child cries out with horror as the fateful moment arrives. The advent of the new governess and the first day in the schoolroom were as much to be dreaded as the first day in a new boarding school for a child who has never left home. Surely Eleanor Farjeon's mother must have realized that when she played a cruel joke on her own children:

> One day a sinister figure mounted the stairs and came to the nursery door; a thin queer formless figure draped in black, with a shapeless hat swathed in a heavy veil that darkened the visitor's features, and black kid gloves protruding from a strange mantle. Visitor? Rather a visitant wandered out of a bad dream. It stood in the doorway, announcing in a squeaky voice: 'Well, dear children! I'm the New Governess.'
>
> We stood appalled.
>
> The Creature minced into the nursery. A howl rent the air and Bertie burst into tears.
>
> Shaking with merriment the figure flew at him open-armed. Light flashed upon me; I darted at the horrid image, tore the veil from its face and screamed, 'It's all right; Bertie! it's all right! It's Mama!'
>
> *A Nursery in the Nineties*, ELEANOR FARJEON

Poor children! There is no doubt that, for a moment, they believed that the 'sinister figure' was, in fact, their new governess; not because they did not know what governesses looked like – their friends had governesses – but because they did.

The Victorian governess was often a very sad creature indeed. The whole system of female education in the nineteenth century fitted a girl for one thing and one thing only – marriage. Those

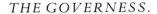
many unfortunate women who never caught a husband and yet who were too well-born to work manually had but two options open to them. They could either take in sewing or something of the sort, or they could teach. Many – far too many – took the latter course and the consequence was that there were too many governesses chasing far too few positions. Desperate for a job and a roof over their heads governesses were prepared to work for pitiful wages. A girl who had been trained to teach at an institution like the 'Clergy Orphan School' or 'St Mary's Hall' in Brighton could command a salary of £100 per annum in the 1840s. But she would be lucky to get it when there were a score of applicants all after the same job who were prepared to accept one-tenth of that sum. If she were lucky enough to find a position, she could easily find herself earning less than the cook and having to perform all sorts of menial tasks in addition to her schoolroom duties. The Rev. Anthony Thomson writing in 1865 was one of the many who inveighed against the system:

> What must a governess be? The word 'lady' hardly expresses the accomplishments she must possess. It is a hard fate to be an angel of virtue, propriety, and piety, combining therewith a knowledge of almost everything, yet having no repugnance to mending stockings, and to be paid for the exhibition of this standing miracle with £20 per annum! Let us hope that the ridicule and satire that has been heaped on the monstrous cheap governess system, has gone some way to disabuse the minds of many worthy people who have been dull to all serious remonstrance as to the shameful injury which, by the perpetuation of such a system, they not only inflict on the admirable women who form the class of governesses, but on their own children. Half the evils of modern female education are traceable to the impossible requirements made on gover-nesses, which all end in delusion and vexation, and necessitate the remedies known as 'Ladies' College' and the 'Finishing

THE GOVERNESS.

Too young for the schoolroom – the governess is introduced to the youngest member of the family.

School', with their troops of 'masters and professors', or, in some cases, the 'convent' abroad.

But the position did not change. In the 1840s over one hundred governesses advertised daily in *The Times* and the average wage asked was between £20 and £40 per annum. By 1850 there were 21,000 governesses registered in London, and even at the end of the century this pathetic advertisement appeared with hundreds like it in *The Lady:*

> Nursery-governess, about twenty-seven, for four children. Usual English subjects; good needlewoman; musical; able to take entire charge; photo; – Bank House, Faringdon (£20).
>
> *The Lady*, 2 January 1897

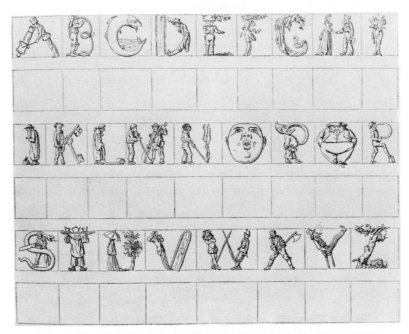

A page from a child's copy-book of the 1870s. The standard of ingenuity of design is remarkable.

'A Apple Pie' – the younger inhabitants of the schoolroom could not fail to identify with the children in this illustration to the famous Victorian alphabet mnemonic.

As if things were not bad enough, there became an increasing vogue towards the end of the nineteenth century for foreign governesses, fraüleins and ma'mselles:

'A German-Swiss governess can be highly recommended; teaching English thoroughly, music (not a brilliant performer), French and Italian. A highly cultivated person – apply: Hon. Mrs Parker, Eccleston, CHESTER.   ibid.

How was the Victorian mother to choose a suitable candidate for the post of governess to her children? There were always plenty of people ready to advise her:

Any one exercising authority over the minds of little folks should be, in the most literal sense of the word, a superior person. A governess should not only be thoroughly conversant with the subjects she professes to teach, but she should be an example to the children under her charge – in conduct, deportment, and general personal habits. Many things in life tend to efface the book-learning we acquire in childhood; but the example of our elders and teachers is rarely forgotten. The manner of viewing the ordinary affairs of life, the interpretation we give to inexplicable facts, the prejudices which influence our judgment in mature years, may all be prompted by the unwritten lessons we learnt from simple contact with a refined or vulgar mind – an educated, or intellectual person, as the case might be.

It is not reasonable to expect that a very desirable teacher can be found without considerable search. Superior abilities in followers of every calling of life are the exception, not the rule. If difficulty is experienced in selecting proficients in mechanical arts, how greatly is the task increased when the more subtle distinctions of mental qualifications are in question! Judging from external appearances, numberless eligible teachers may be found on every side. Style of dress and pleasing manners are very much the effect of the prevailing taste of the day, and are adopted accordingly; but a peculiar cast of mind is not so easily discerned. It is only by intimate acquaintance that one is enabled to discover the inner-self of those with whom we associate.

In engaging a governess, something more than the stereotyped list of questions which are addressed to a domestic servant when applying for a situation, is needful. Some certainty of knowledge that the candidate really possesses fitness for her post is necessary. This certainty can hardly be expected to result from an interview of a few minutes' duration, such as is customary to bestow at an agent's office, or on the introduction of a chance go-between. The best mode of engaging a governess is through private recommendation. People, of whom the circumstances, family and connections, are known on either side, are likely to be more congenial to each other than strangers. A feeling of semi-friendship is the usual result of such acquaintance, and is altogether the most happy auspice under which similar relations can be formed. The children themselves are no less benefited by the favourable circumstance than the employer and employed.

Having succeeded in finding a desirable instructress of approved principles and acquirements, the question of salary should be decided in liberal spirit. A common sense of justice should prompt this course, added to a feeling of humanity, which dictates that we should enable those who serve us in their prime of life to make some provision for old age. People who are not prepared to make a pecuniary sacrifice on this account, can hardly expect entire devotedness on the part of those who serve them.

Cassell's Household Guide

It is small wonder that the profession of governess did not often appeal to the most attractive women. For a miserable salary they had to be able to teach all aspects of English, French, German and Italian; singing, music, painting in oils and water-

ONE, TWO.

1. 2.
3. 4.
5. 6.
7. 8.
9. 10.
11. 12.
13. 14.

One, two,
Buckle my shoe;

Three, four,
Knock at the door;

Five, six,
Pick up sticks;

Seven, eight,
Lay them straight;

Nine, ten,
A good fat hen;

Eleven, twelve,
Who will delve;

Thirteen, fourteen,
Maids a-courting;

256

Lessons made easy – the favourite numbers rhyme which has made learning to count easier for generations of children is illustrated here by the Victorian artist, Charles Robinson.

15.16.
17.18.
19.20.

Fifteen, sixteen,
Maids in the kitchen;

Seventeen, eighteen,
Maids a-waiting;

Nineteen, twenty,
My plate's empty.

257

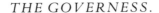
colours, pencil and chalk drawing, ornamental needlework,
geography, history, divinity, mathematics and dancing. In addition they were expected to have a good moral influence on their
charges, teaching them manners and deportment and generally
preparing them for adulthood. They were instantly dismissable
in the event of any real or imagined misdemeanour and more
often than not had to run the gauntlet between a tyrannical
nanny, an hysterical mother and ungovernable children. It was as
rare to find a governess who stayed with one family for more
than a year as it was to find a nurse who didn't.

Alice Pollock in her autobiography *Portrait of My Victorian
Youth* remembers her governesses very clearly. First there was a
Miss Taylor who was strict but popular. She became ill and died.
Then there was Miss Mew who married (appropriately a Mr
Catt!). Miss Mew was followed by a French governess who was
dismissed on account of her bad character. Miss de la Valette
followed her. She could not control the children and handed in
her notice. Finally a German governess arrived – a Miss Iseke:

> We detested her. Unfortunately she attained a great deal of
> influence over our mother, and made mischief between her
> and us . . . Miss Iseke punished us a good deal, and Eleanor was
> subjected to much severer punishment than the rest of the
> family. I think Miss Iseke disliked her, and made mischief
> between her and Mother. On one occasion she persuaded her
> to have Eleanor locked in her room, which was an attic and
> cold. She was to be fed on bread and water for a week and to
> see no one. She became ill and the doctor had to be sent for.
> On enquiry as to what had happened, he was furious, ordering
> her to be put to bed and kept warm, and to be given good
> food. One lung was slightly touched . . .
>
> As Miss Iseke's influence increased with Mother, we saw
> less of her. Miss Iseke was always trying to take the position of
> eldest daughter of the house. We always called Mother

'Mum', and to our great rage Miss Iseke called her
'Mumchen'.

Miss Pollock goes on to tell how Miss Iseke eventually became
her mother's companion and stayed with her until she died.

    This rather macabre story is interesting in that it shows the
essential weakness of the governess's position. Although few
women would have gone to Miss Iseke's lengths to ensure their
security. Most governesses were rather pathetic creatures –
occasionally an object of terror to their charges, but more often a
source of amusement to adults and children alike. Few were
loved as nannies were loved and very few were of the stature of
the Brontë sisters. It is therefore rather refreshing to find a

The violin lesson – a good governess was expected to be able to teach music as
well as being able to acquit herself adequately at the piano.

VOCABULAIRE SYMBOLIQUE ANGLO-FRANÇAIS.

LA SALLE À MANGER—THE DINING-ROOM.

Un Plateau. / A Tea-tray.

Une Théière. / A Tea-pot.

Une Cafetière. / A Coffee-pot.

Une Tasse. / A Cup.

Une Soucoupe. / A Saucer.

Bol au Dépôt. / A Slop Basin.

Un Bol. / A Bowl.

Un Sucrier. / A Sugar-basin.

Une Pince à Sucre. / Sugar-tongs.

Un Coquetier. / An Egg-cup.

Un Crémier. / A Cream-jug.

Une Soupière. / A Soup-tureen.

Un Plat. / A Dish.

Une Assiette. / A Plate.

Une Saucière. / A Sauce Boat.

Un Saladier. / A Salad Bowl.

Un Pot à Eau. / A Ewer.

Un Moutardier. / A Mustard-pot.

Une Salière. / A Salt-cellar.

Un Huilier. / A Cruet-stand. Une Burette. / A Cruet.

Une Carafe. / A Decanter.

Un Carafon. / Small Decanter.

Bouchon—Stopper.

Une Bouteille. / A Bottle.

Un Tire-bouchon. / A Corkscrew.

Un Gobelet. / Goblet, Mug.

Une Timbale. / Silver Drinking-cup.

Un Verre. / A Glass.

Un Verre à Pied. / A Tumbler.

Un Verre à Liqueur. / A Wine Glass.

Une Serviette. / A Table Napkin. Une Coulant de Serviette. / A Napkin Ring.

Un Couteau. / A Knife.

Une Fourchette. / A Fork.

Une Cuiller. / A Spoon.

Une Cuiller à Pot. / A Pot-ladle.

Un Fusil. / A Steel.

Un Casse-noisette. / A pair of Nutcracks.

Un Réchaud de Table. / Dish-warmer.

Une Truelle à Poisson. / A Fish Knife.

Une Corbeille à Pain. / A Bread-basket.

Two pages from a nineteenth-century French vocabulary book. All the objects would have been instantly recognizable to a middle-class child in the 1850s.

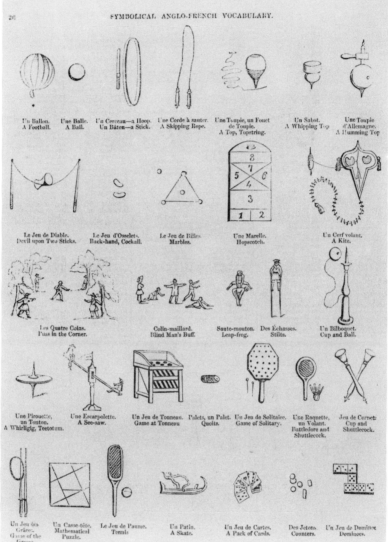

26   SYMBOLICAL ANGLO-FRENCH VOCABULARY.

Un Ballon.
A Football.

Une Balle.
A Ball.

Un Cerceau—a Hoop.
Un Bâton—a Stick.

Une Corde à sauter.
A Skipping Rope.

Une Toupie, un Fouet
de Toupie.
A Top, Topstring.

Un Sabot.
A Whipping Top.

Une Toupie
d'Allemagne.
A Humming Top

Le Jeu de Diable.
Devil upon Two Sticks.

Le Jeu d'Osselets.
Back-hand, Cockall.

Le Jeu de Billes.
Marbles.

Une Marelle.
Hopscotch.

Un Cerf volant.
A Kite.

Les Quatre Coins.
Puss in the Corner.

Colin-maillard.
Blind Man's Buff.

Saute-mouton.
Leap-frog.

Des Échasses.
Stilts.

Un Bilboquet.
Cup and Ball.

Une Pirouette,
un Tonton.
A Whirligig, Teetotum.

Une Escarpolette.
A See-saw.

Un Jeu de Tonneau.
Game at Tonneau.

Palets, un Palet.
Quoits.

Un Jeu de Solitaire.
Game of Solitary.

Une Raquette,
un Volant.
Battledore and
Shuttlecock.

Jeu de Cornet:
Cup and
Shuttlecock.

Un Jeu des
Grâces.
Game of the
Graces.

Un Casse-tête.
Mathematical
Puzzle.

Le Jeu de Paume.
Tennis

Un Patin.
A Skate.

Un Jeu de Cartes.
A Pack of Cards.

Des Jetons.
Counters.

Un Jeu de Dominos.
Dominoes.

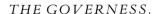

'special' one: Miss Cutting was Lady Lubbock's governess, who stayed with her throughout her girlhood and even accompanied her on a cycling tour of the Rhineland. As they return home there is a rather touching scene:

> At last we sat on the steamer's deck, in perfect weather, watching the green leas and the neat houses of Folkestone approach us. I felt with a sudden pang that this was the end of something irretrievable, the close of a chapter. I turned to Scutty, 'Oh, dear, I *am* going to miss you so,' I said, and clutched her hand.
>
> But she disengaged it gently. 'My dear, don't distress yourself,' she said with her usual composure. 'I don't think you *will* miss me very much, though it is natural for you to think so. Your life is beginning. You will find new friends and new interests. You will have little time to miss anyone. But *I* shall miss *you*, for life is not opening but closing in, as is natural at my age, and I shall be very glad whenever you find time to write to me.'

THE TREATS.

I WOKE before the morning, I was happy all the day,
I never said an ugly word, but smiled and stuck to play.

'A Good Boy', ROBERT LOUIS STEVENSON

SCHOOLROOM days were not all dull days. The Victorian child, unlike the child of other ages, lived in a very special world that was geared to his or her needs. All work and no play was by no means the rule of a nineteenth-century childhood. In fact Victorian educationalists were unanimous in their statements about the importance of 'constructive recreation'. Playing was a way of learning and even keeping pets became a vehicle for teaching children about animals in the most charming way. Any Victorian boy who wanted to know what his pet white mice should be fed on, would have found the answer in Mrs Valentine's *Home Book of Pleasure and Instruction*. But he would also have found a great deal more information that was eminently readable:

> Squirrels, Dormice, and White Mice are sometimes kept in captivity by English girls, whose lives are chiefly spent in towns, and who have no knowledge of the wild frolicsome creatures in their native haunts; but they appear to lead very unnatural lives in confinement, and are not very desirable pets for the house: it is difficult to keep their cages quite sweet and clean. All may be domesticated, however, and are, I believe, capable of attachment to their owners. I have never kept any myself; but my brothers had dormice from time to time, and several small families were born and brought up under their care, but most of them came to an untimely end.
>
> The Squirrel seems so delightfully free and happy, playing

The pet rabbit – the English love of animals was handed down to their children by nineteenth-century parents who encouraged the keeping of pets.

about on the tops of the tallest trees in the woods, launching himself boldly into the air, and taking tremendous leaps from branch to branch, that after seeing the pretty little creature at his ease, one does not feel inclined to deprive him of the liberty he seems so thoroughly to enjoy; but if he is captured, his life ought to be made as happy as possible, and he should be

Victorian sentimentality reached unparalleled heights in its treatment of children with animals.

allowed as much exercise as he can have in the house. His cage should be at least 3 or 4 feet long and 3 or 4 feet high, and instead of the revolving cylinder, which is very injurious to the little prisoner, he should have a good-sized branch of a tree, to form perches for him, and be able to frisk about at pleasure in his little parlour. A little sleeping-box must be attached to this, with a door at the back, and the board forming the floor should be drawn out like that of a bird-cage. Every part of the cage must be kept as clean as possible, and the moss and cotton wool, which must be put into the squirrel's bedroom, must be changed nearly every day. The active little creature does not often live long in confinement; but if taken young, and very carefully managed, it may become a very tame, and very engaging pet, and may sometimes be trusted to frolic about out of doors when tame enough to return at his mistress's call. His cage should, however, be lined with tin; for he is apt to gnaw the wood with his sharp little teeth when impatient of confinement. He should be fed on nuts, almonds, filberts, beechmasts, walnuts, acorns, wheat in the ear, and fir cones; and he is fond of milk, cold tea, and bread and milk. A little bit of boiled potato, and even a tiny morsel of cooked meat, may be given as a treat, and a stale crust of bread to gnaw. All creatures require variety in their food, and in his wild state the squirrel gets animal food by robbing birds' nests of their eggs occasionally. He lays up a store of food for the winter in various holes and crevices, and is much too acute ever to put by a nut in which a maggot has been, or to miss the place where his treasure is concealed, even when several inches deep of snow cover the ground. The female is a very affectionate mother, and will remain with her young in the nest even while the tree in which it is is cut down, or will carry them, one after another, in her mouth, to a place of safety. She generally builds on the topmost branches of the fir tree, and the nest is made of dry grass and sticks, very slightly yet firmly put together, and lined with fur, which she scratches off her body before the young ones are born. This is generally in the summer, and the young squirrels remain with their parents till the following spring, when they are able to manage for themselves. They have a substantial winter's nest, to which they appear to add every year fresh layers of hay and moss, to make their habitation more and more warm and comfortable. I have been told that the best time to buy a squirrel is at the end of September, when it is fat and vigorous and its fur is in good condition; but it is never safe to purchase those which are sold in the street as 'wonderfully tame', and which will allow themselves to be handled by a stranger, and pulled about, without showing any disposition to bite. The probability is that the poor little creatures have been stupefied by some drug, and that they will either recover their natural

A romantic view of Victorian girls gathering blackberries.

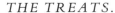
ferocity in a few hours, or die – poisoned by the narcotic
which has been given them . . .

   White, grey and white and brown and white mice are
sometimes kept in cages like those of the dormouse, and they
must be treated in the same manner. The common brown
mouse is said to be a more tractable and intelligent pet, and to
be easily tamed by patient kindness. I never heard a mouse
sing, but several instances are recorded of mice who have
learned to imitate the chirp and even the song of a canary kept
in the room in which they were; so that it might be worth-
while to try to give such pets the benefit of a musical education
for the chance of their acquiring so curious an accomplish-
ment.

On a particularly fine day the governess might just be pre-
vailed upon to take her charges on a picnic. Fresh air and exercise

'Oranges and Lemons' – this game, still popular with children today, was
known to Victorians as 'The Chimes'. These country children could not be
happier.

Playing trains – the original caption to this drawing reads: 'Don't tell Tommy he's only a truck!' The artist is du Maurier.

were especially highly regarded by governesses and parents alike and after the obligatory botany, there would certainly be time for recreation:

> Spring is the time for playing out of doors – on the green smooth lawn, in the garden or in the meadows. How pleasant it is to gather daisies, and make them into chains or balls, sitting on the grass, with the bright sun shining on the tender green of the trees, and the lark singing high up in the blue sky . . .
>
> 'Let us have a game of the Silly Shepherdess,' said little Fanny.
>
> 'How do you play it?' asked her cousin Katie, who was staying with them.
>
> 'Oh, we will show you! Philip shall be a wolf, and I will be a shepherdess. All of you are to be my sheep. Now take hands,

all six of you, and stand closely side by side, shoulder to shoulder with your arms down by your sides. Philip will hide behind the laurels. Now I take a stick, which I must call my crook, and I measure how long a string you make, *instead of counting you*; that's why I am called a *silly* shepherdess. I must see how many sticks or crooks you are long. Now I must go away and Ada will show you what to do next.'

Fanny then ran off, sat down on the bench under the oak tree, and pretended to go to sleep.

'Sister lambs,' said Ada, in a whisper, 'I think I should like

The horrors of sea bathing – the early nineteenth century saw an enormous growth of interest in sea bathing, and the establishment of that formidable figure the bathing woman. This young Victorian is not a devotee of the new vogue.

(182)

Seaside holidays became fashionable in the Victorian era and coastal resorts flourished. It seems obvious from the expression on these children's faces that their holiday is coming to an end.

to have a little run outside the fold. If the shepherdess should come while I am gone, will you try to prevent her from finding out that I am not here?'

All the lambs answered, 'Yes we will try.'

Then Ada ran away, and danced and jumped about like a little frolicking lamb. But very soon Philip (who made a capital wolf) sprang from behind his tree, and carried her off with him to his den.

And now Fanny woke up; and when the lambs saw her coming, the two end ones stretched out their arms as far as they could; 'For,' they said, 'two arms' length will be wider even than our sister lamb was.'

The silly shepherdess measured her lambs again. When she had finished doing so, she said,

'This is wonderful! they have grown since I went to sleep; they are a little longer.' . . .

Meeting the gillie – after the Royal Family had 'discovered' Scotland
in the 1850s, it became more and more fashionable for holidays.

This sort of play went on until so many lambs were gone, or
had been taken by the wolf, that only two were left. Then they
only put the tips of their fingers together, and stretched out
their arms, to deceive the shepherdess. But as they could not,
even thus, make six sticks in length, the silly shepherdess
guessed what had happened, and went in search of the wolf.

'Wolf! wolf!' she cried, 'give me back my lambs!'

'Shepherdess, you shall have them if you can catch them,'
said the wolf. And he let all the lambs out of his den. The
shepherdess ran after them. While she was gone, the cunning
wolf stole the two lambs left. When at last the shepherdess

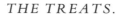

caught a lamb, it became 'Shepherdess' instead, and the game began over again.

The picture of those Victorian children playing 'The Silly Shepherdess' in the open-air is irresistible and probably far too good to be true. But the best day, by far, for Victorian children was the first day of the summer holidays when lessons were temporarily given up in favour of pure unfettered enjoyment. There could be picnics every day. Many families, too, were used to taking an annual seaside holiday at this time. The Queen had first bathed in the sea on 30 July 1847:

> Drove down to the beach with my maid and went into the bathing machine, where I undressed and bathed in the sea (for the first time in my life), a very nice bathing woman attending me. I thought it was delightful until I put my head under the water, when I thought I should be stifled.

As in so many other things, what the Royal Family did on holiday became immediately fashionable. Seaside resorts sprang up all around the coast. Where there had once only been fishermen's cottages, there were suddenly towns with amusements and shops on every side. If Victorian adults enjoyed themselves, that was nothing to what the children did:

> Amid the wave-beat rocks the children play,
> Their white feet sparkle in the foamy spray:
> O shining sea, till sinks the happy day,
> The children seek thy side.
>
> Until the golden cloudless hours be done,
> To cull thy shells the lads and lassies run;
> They laugh to see thee dimple in the sun,
> And spread thine arms so wide.
>
> They watch the sails that bird-like fly away
> Across the rippling waters of the bay;

THE TREATS.

For harvest of the sea the fishers stray
Far out across the tide.

And when the boats come home with silver store,
The little footsteps gather to the shore:
O sunlit sea, thy charms seem never o'er –
What joys around thee hide!

Behold the stately castles, firm and tall,
Reared up in sand by willing hands so small,
At morn, at noon, still busy one and all,
To raise those halls of pride!

O glorious sea, ring out in deathless lay,
What though the bairnies' castles fall away,
The children have a Dwelling-place for aye –
God's love doth strong abide.

By the Deep Sea, M.S. HAYCRAFT (1891)

With the party season in full swing, the children are introduced to one of
the guests at their parents' dinner party.

This cartoon of two boys looking in on an adults' party has the caption:
'I say – let's change all the numbers! . . .' (they do it!) It appeared in 1885.

And even when the summer holiday was over and the dreaded
schoolroom lessons had started again, there was still Christmas
to long for. Christmas meant presents and parties:

> Four hours are the usual limits of a child's party, and it is
> injudicious to attempt to crowd too great a variety of amuse-
> ments into this space of time, as the programme must, in such
> a case, be hurriedly gone through to be fully completed before
> the hour of departure.

(187)

THE TREATS.

Afternoon juvenile parties take place from 4 to 7; evening juvenile parties from 6 to 10.

It is usual to provide some special amusement for children apart from games and dancing.

The 'conjurer' is always in request, and the charge for an exhibition of conjuring varies from one to five guineas.

In town the newest amusements are readily obtainable, in addition to such old favourites as marionettes, Punch and Judy, performing dogs, performing birds, etc., etc. The cost of hire of either of the above ranges from two to ten guineas.

Boisterous games or games in which children of all ages can join never fail to amuse; but it is generally found that if prolonged beyond an hour, the younger children become tired and cross, the older boys obstreperous and unmanageable, while the little girls either loudly complain of the rough play of the boys, or take refuge in tears, at which the mammas present are very much concerned.

It much depends upon the ages of the children whether dancing is the chief feature at a juvenile party, or whether it is only limited to one hour. If the majority of the children are boys, they prefer any description of amusement to dancing; if the contrary is the case the little girls are generally found willing to dance as long as any one is willing to play for them. Generally the governess, or one of the members of the family undertakes the musical arrangements, otherwise a professional pianist is engaged to play the piano; the cost of whose services averages from fifteen shillings to one guinea. A piano is considered sufficient at juvenile parties without the addition of any other instrument.

Soon after the arrival of the children at a juvenile party, they are taken down into the dining-room to have tea; if space permits seats are provided for all; if not, the earliest arrivals are sent in to tea without delay, and are followed in their turn by later arrivals.

For a party of fifty children the following quantities would

The children have just arrived at a party and are being smartened up before going in to tea.

The little Iron Duke – children's party costume became so extravagant in the 1880s that almost anything might have come through the door.

be consumed: – 1 gallon of tea; from ½ a gallon to 1 gallon of coffee; hot and cold milk, 5 quarts; of sugar, 4 lbs would be provided. Twelve plates of thin bread and butter, three plum or currant cakes, two rice cakes, 4 lbs of various kinds of biscuits, 2½ dozen sponge cakes, 4 dozen small buns. When fruit is not in season, preserve or honey is often given at a children's tea party, either strawberry, raspberry or gooseberry jam.

The tea-table should be entirely covered with a white table-cloth. Tea and coffee cups are placed on a tea-tray at either end, and dishes of eatables are placed down the centre of the table.

The governess of the family, assisted by one or more of the grown-up daughters, pours out the tea or coffee, and the women-servants are in attendance to supply the children with all they may require, overlooked and assisted by the ladies present.

Queuing up for the conjurer – at Victorian children's parties it was usual always to have a professional entertainer to share the responsibility of keeping the guests amused.

'We had crackers' – a boy and his three sisters have just arrived back from a
children's party and are telling their mother all about it.

When a juvenile party is given, from 25 to 30 grown-up
people are usually asked – the relatives of the children – who
either accompany them or arrive shortly after tea, and for
whom a small supper is provided, served at half-past seven,
before the departure of the children.

And so the party ended, the day ended and the year ended and
the Victorian child was one year nearer that half longed-for, half
dreaded day when he or she would make the seemingly endless
climb down the stairs to take a rightful place in adult society.

When that day came there would be no more nursery, no more
schoolroom; no more castor oil and no more *Otto's German
Grammar*. There would be no more nurse and no more excuses.
The Victorian child was used to transitions; from mother to
nurse; from nursery to schoolroom. Would this last one be as

traumatic? Was the Victorian childhood a preparation for life?

Time alone would tell. But one thing was certain – a child with a loving nurse and an intelligent governess would always look back on that attic childhood with gratitude and affection and would probably be none the worse for having had a few years of that 'pretend' life which was the reality of the Victorian Nursery.

Summer afternoon – one of the older children sits daydreaming by the nursery window. Above her head is an illuminated biblical text which she can doubtless recite from memory.

(192)